Bloom's Modern Critical Interpretations

Bloom's Modern Critical Interpretations

F. Scott Fitzgerald's
Short Stories

Edited and with an introduction by
Harold Bloom
Sterling Professor of the Humanities
Yale University

BLOOM'S
LITERARY CRITICISM
An Infobase Learning Company

Bloom's Modern Critical Interpretations: F. Scott Fitzgerald's Short Stories

Copyright © 2011 by Infobase Learning

Introduction © 2011 by Harold Bloom

Bloom's Literary Criticism
An imprint of Infobase Publishing
132 West 31st Street
New York NY 10001

Library of Congress Cataloging-in-Publication Data
F. Scott Fitzgerald's short stories / edited and with an introduction by Harold Bloom.
    p. cm.—(Bloom's modern critical interpretations)
Includes bibliographical references and index.
ISBN 978-1-60413-273-1
1. Fitzgerald, F. Scott (Francis Scott), 1896–1940—Criticism and interpretation.   2. Short story.   I. Bloom, Harold.
PS3511.I9Z6165 2011
813'.52—dc22
                                    2011012813

Contributing editor: Pamela Loos
Cover design by Alicia Post
Composition by IBT Global, Troy NY
Cover printed by Yurchak Printing, Landisville PA
Book printed and bound by Yurchak Printing, Landisville PA
Date printed: August 2011
Printed in the United States of America

10 9 8 7 6 5 4 3 2 1

Contents

Editor's Note

My introduction centers on the beautiful story "Winter Dreams," which I relate both to the endless influence of John Keats on Fitzgerald and to *The Great Gatsby*, Fitzgerald's Keatsian (and Conradian) masterpiece.

Fitzgerald remarked that the archetypes of his myth were Cinderella and Prince Charming, a dialectic explored by Kenneth G. Johnston's analysis of "Crazy Sunday."

As a Keatsian, lyrical storyteller, Fitzgerald relied on his genius for metaphor, which is the subject of William J. Brondell's essay.

Leonard A. Podis juxtaposes "The Diamond as Big as the Ritz" with Hawthorne's splendidly sinister "Rappaccini's Daughter," while Robert Roulston meditates the dubious responsibilities of "May Day."

Keats returns in Bruce L. Grenberg's examination of "Outside the Cabinet-Maker's," after which J. Gerald Kennedy brings together the two friendly rivals, Fitzgerald and Hemingway, in a contrast between "Babylon Revisited" and "The Snows of Kilimanjaro."

A further range of "Babylon Revisited" is traversed by Richard Allan Davison, while Veronica Makowsky contrasts Faulkner and Fitzgerald in their studies of southern nostalgias.

Two apt summings-up conclude this volume: Ronald Berman on what Gertrude Stein would have called "the geographical history of America" in Fitzgerald and Scott Donaldson on the central thematic of marriage and money.

HAROLD BLOOM

Introduction

Amid the God's plenty of Scott Fitzgerald's stories, each of us may have particular favorites. Mine is "Winter Dreams," written in the *annus mirabilis* of 1922, when Joyce's *Ulysses* and Eliot's "The Waste Land" were published, soon after to be followed by the *Harmonium* of Wallace Stevens in 1923 and Hart Crane's *White Buildings* in 1926.

In the perspective of nearly a century, these works of high modernism all can be seen as late romantic descendants of the dreams of transcendent love in Shelley and Keats. Joyce, like Beckett after him, was Shelley haunted, as was Hart Crane. Eliot and Stevens may seem antithetical to one another in this, since Eliot concealed his roots in Shelley, Tennyson, and Walt Whitman, while Stevens did not. But the lineage of Shelley's remorseless quest for a perfect love embraces all these, as it does also Browning, Hardy, Yeats, and Virginia Woolf.

The dream of love in John Keats has a Shelleyan aspect, yet there is less Plato in Keats and more David Hume, as it were. Shelley's skepticism was more philosophical than erotic, while no eros surpasses Keats's clear sense of the limited nature of dream and of desire. The great odes and *The Eve of Saint Agnes* always reverberated in Scott Fitzgerald's heart and mind, and "Winter Dreams" can be read as a prose poem on the death of the erotic imagination.

Three years later, *The Great Gatsby* developed magnificently the vision of "Winter Dreams," whose Dexter Green falls in love with the idea of Judy Jones, as inadequate a human being as Gatsby's Daisy. Matthew J. Bruccoli wisely points to the conclusion of "Winter Dreams" as Dexter's grief "for the loss of his capacity to grieve":

He had thought that having nothing else to lose he was invulnerable at last—but he knew that he had just lost something more, as surely as if he had married Judy Jones and seen her fade away before his eyes.

The dream was gone. Something had been taken from him. In a sort of panic he pushed the palms of his hands into his eyes and tried to bring up a picture of the waters lapping on Sherry Island and the moonlit veranda, and gingham on the golf-links and the dry sun and the gold color of her neck's soft down. And her mouth damp to his kisses and her eyes plaintive with melancholy and her freshness like new fine linen in the morning. Why, these things were no longer in the world! They had existed and they existed no longer.

For the first time in years the tears were streaming down his face. But they were for himself now. He did not care about mouth and eyes and moving hands. He wanted to care, and he could not care. For he had gone away and he could never go back any more. The gates were closed, the sun was gone down, and there was no beauty but the gray beauty of steel that withstands all time. Even the grief he could have borne was left behind in the country of illusion, of youth, of the richness of life, where his winter dreams had flourished.

"Long ago," he said, "long ago, there was something in me, but now that thing is gone. Now that thing is gone, that thing is gone. I cannot cry. I cannot care. That thing will come back no more."

Wonderfully phrased, that carried the authority of late romantic tradition from Keats on to the visions of loss in William Butler Yeats. When the capacity for intense feeling departs, the quester loses not the desired object but something vital and irrevocable in the self.

KENNETH G. JOHNSTON

Fitzgerald's "Crazy Sunday":
Cinderella in Hollywood

"Alice and Cinderella are most real."

—Karl Shapiro, "Hollywood"

"The two basic stories of all times," wrote F. Scott Fitzgerald, "are *Cinderella* and *Jack the Giant Killer*—the charm of women and the courage of men."[1] His own fiction is clearly identified with the first. Beckoned by the charm and glitter of golden girls, his "cinder-lads" dream of shedding the rags of their drab existences and of gaining entry into the romantic world symbolized by the Prince's ball in the fairytale. After 1930, however, Fitzgerald's work reflects an increasing concern with the return to the ashes, with the period after the magic hour has struck. With varying degrees of emphases, Fitzgerald told his basic story, or parts of it, again and again. "Mostly, we authors must repeat ourselves," he admitted, "—that's the truth."[2]

"Crazy Sunday," which was first published in the *American Mercury* in 1932, is yet another variation of the Cinderella tale. The cast includes a beautiful actress with golden hair; a motion-picture director whose "'magical'" touch has "'brought that little gamin alive and made her a sort of masterpiece'"[3]; and a handsome young man who falls in love with the little gamin, a former bit player. In the climactic scene, a clock strikes "in trumpet notes. *Nine-ten-eleven-twelve*—" (p. 187). The central focus of Fitzgerald's story,

From *Literature/Film Quarterly* 6 (1978): 214–21. Copyright © 1978 by Salisbury University.

3

however, is not on the Cinderella character, but rather on a Hollywood script writer who, as the story opens, has just been invited to a "top-drawer" party at "Cinderella's" lavish home in Beverly Hills.

Fitzgerald thought that "Crazy Sunday" was "a fine story,"[4] but when he submitted it to the *Saturday Evening Post*, it was rejected on the grounds that "it didn't get anywhere or prove anything." The editors of the magazine, reported Fitzgerald's agent, conceded that it "was beautifully written and a very accurate picture of Hollywood"; moreover, they liked the beginning of the story very much. But they "didn't think the tragedy at the end was prepared for or essentially a part of the story."[5] In recent years the critical response to "Crazy Sunday" has varied widely. Andrew Turnbull calls the story "masterly," and Arthur Mizener ranks it among Fitzgerald's "best work."[6] But others treat it as a footnote to Fitzgerald's second Hollywood visit; or misread it as a confused tribute to Irving Thalberg, the young production genius at the Metro-Goldwyn-Mayer studio; or fault it for characterization and structure. Fitzgerald did make a "'jackass'" of himself at a party given by Thalberg and his actress-wife, Norma Shearer, at their Malibu beach home in late 1931.[7] But Turnbull is quite right when he declares that "'Crazy Sunday' cuts deeper than Fitzgerald's private humiliation."[8] The fact that Thalberg was the real-life model for both Miles Calman in "Crazy Sunday" and Monroe Stahr in *The Last Tycoon* has also blurred some critical insights. Henry Dan Piper, for instance, views Calman as "the hero" of "Crazy Sunday" and insists that the story revolves about Fitzgerald's "mixed feelings of admiration and dislike" for Thalberg. Piper, however, finds it "impossible to reconcile the charming Stella Walker of the first part of the story with the brassy nymphomaniac she has become at the end." Thus he believes that "'Crazy Sunday' fails as a work of fiction."[9] Sergio Perosa also sees the story as flawed: "Fitzgerald has not clarified his attitude toward his characters. The exact relationships between them are not properly explained, their motivations are obscure, and their merits and defects are not clearly indicated. There is also a structural disharmony between the first part of the story, which is rather humorous, and the second part."[10] Actually, Perosa's remarks, which are reminiscent of the early *Post* criticism, should be leveled at Joel Coles, not at F. Scott Fitzgerald. For "Crazy Sunday" is an excellent story, skillfully conceived and executed, and the "shortcomings," of which Perosa and Piper complain, stem from the limitations of the narrator.

The key to "Crazy Sunday," then, is its point of view. Joel Coles provides the focus of narration, but at the very outset his trustworthiness—that is, his ability to distinguish between appearance and reality—is called into question: the son of a successful actress, "Joel had spent his childhood between London and New York trying to separate the real from the unreal, or at least to keep one guess ahead" (p. 172). As a grown man, he is still trying, but without much success; herein lies the major source of dramatic irony which pervades "Crazy Sunday." By using an unreliable narrator, who is also the central character, Fitzgerald invites one to look behind and beyond Joel's explanations and perceptions, while at the same time permitting the reader to participate in, even to enjoy, at first hand the excitement and glamour of several Hollywood parties. The final effect is what Malcolm Cowley has called "double vision":

> Fitzgerald lived in his great moments, and lived in them again when he remembered their drama; but he also stood apart from them and coldly reckoned their causes and consequences. That is his doubleness or irony and it is one of his distinguishing marks as a writer. He took part in the ritual orgies of his time, but he also kept a secretly detached position. . . . Always he cultivated a double vision. . . . It was as if all his stories described a big dance to which he had taken . . . the prettiest girl . . . and as if at the same time he stood outside the ballroom, a little Midwestern boy with his nose to the glass, wondering how much the tickets cost and who paid for the music. But it was not a dance he was watching so much as it was a drama of conflicting manners and aspirations in which he was both the audience and the leading actor. As audience he kept a cold eye on the actor's performance.[11]

In "Crazy Sunday" Fitzgerald has his eye on Joel Coles. It is Joel's blunted and uncertain perception which is responsible for the inconsistent portrayal of character, the blurred relationships and motivations, and the "structural disharmony." These "shortcomings" reflect flaws in his own character and, thus, they eventually lead one to the thematic center of the story.

Sunday, according to Joel, is different from the other days of the week. For a few blessed hours, he tells us, the sets and sequences, "the ceaseless compromise," "the clash and strain of many personalities," "the struggles of rival ingenuities," are left behind (p. 172). But as the story unfolds, it becomes clear to the reader that Sunday is remarkably like the other days at the studio.

"Crazy Sunday" begins with a Sunday afternoon "tea" at the home of Miles Calman, the director. It is a gathering of important figures and personalities from the motion picture world: writers, actors, actresses, and money men. The Calman mansion provides an appropriate setting: the "house was built for great emotional moments—there was an air of listening, as if the far silences of its vistas hid an audience, but this afternoon it was thronged, as though people had been bidden rather than asked" (p. 173). It is on this stage

that Joel Coles, an ambitious film writer, plans to advance his career by playing the role of "a young man of promise." He even rehearses his part:

> "I won't take anything to drink," he assured himself. Calman
> was audibly tired of rummies, and thought it was a pity the indus-
> try could not get along without them.
>   Joel agreed that writers drank too much—he did himself, but
> he wouldn't this afternoon. He wished Miles would be within
> hearing when the cocktails were passed to hear his succinct,
> unobtrusive, "No, thank you." (p. 173)

Stella Walker Calman does not move on to her other guests after she
speaks to Joel. "She lingered" (p. 173). He pays tribute to her youthful beauty:
"'Well, you look about sixteen! Where's your kiddy car?'" (p. 173). Stella is
visibly pleased. A recent mother, the beautiful actress apparently needs to
be reassured about her charm. "'After a pretty woman has had her first child
. . . ,'" Joel tells her, "'she's got to have some new man's unqualified devotion
to prove to herself she hasn't lost anything'" (p. 174). Nonetheless, Joel is
flattered by her attentions. "She presented several people to Joel *as if* he were
important" (p. 174; italics mine). When she slips a drink into his hand, his
abstemious intentions are compromised. "Reassuring himself that Miles was
at the other side of the room, Joel drank the cocktail" (p. 174). Their conversation is "interrupted at the exact moment Joel would have chosen" (p. 174).
Thus far, Joel is satisfied with the script.

With the party nearly over, Joel, who by now is quite drunk, decides
to perform at center stage. But his performance, a burlesque based upon
the cultural limitations of an independent producer, is by his own admission "'a flop'" (p. 177). It ends in the midst of a confused silence. He feels
the undercurrent of derision; he hears the great screen lover shout "'Boo!
Boo!'" It is "the resentment of the professional toward the amateur, of the
community toward the stranger, the thumbs-down of the clan" (p. 177). He
has "made a fool of himself" before an important group of the picture world,
"upon whose favor depended his career" (p. 176). But Stella Walker whose
radiant smile never vanished throughout the ordeal, thanks him "as if he
had been an unparalleled success." He bows "rather drunkenly" and makes
his exit (p. 177).

The next day Joel awakens to "a broken and ruined world" (p. 177). He
sends the Calmans a note of apology, slinks about the studio like a malefac-
tor, finds a gloomy consolation in staring at some other misfits in the studio restaurant—"the sad, lovely Siamese twins, the mean dwarfs, the proud
giant from the circus picture" (p. 178). Although he vows never again to make

another social appearance in Hollywood, a telegram from Stella the following morning ends his permanent retirement: "'You were one of the most agreeable people at our party. Expect you at my sister June's buffet supper next Sunday'" (p. 178).

The second crazy Sunday is filled with "the clash and strain of many personalities." Miles and Stella arrive, tense and angry, having quarreled fiercely most of the afternoon. Stella has just learned of her husband's affair with her best friend, Eva Goebel. Quivering with shock and emotion, Stella turns to Joel, whose eyes are filled with "unstinted admiration" (p. 179). She sits down "vehemently on the arm of Joel's chair," as though to retaliate for the girl perched "on the arm of Miles's chair" (p. 179). Joel is struck by Stella's natural beauty: he notices "that the mass of her hair was made up of some strands of red gold and some of pale gold, so that it could not be dyed, and that she had on no make-up. She was that good-looking—" (p. 179). When the spectacle of a new girl "hovering" over her husband becomes unbearable, Stella leads Joel into a bedroom, and seated at either end of a big bed, they continue to talk. Miles sticks his head in the room, but Stella goes on talking to Joel as if her husband were not there. Impatiently, Miles suggests that, since his wife had so much to say to Joel, he return home with them.

The scene now shifts back to the theater-like Calman home, where it occurs to Joel that Stella's tears and anger are simply part of a performance.

> Under the high ceilings the situation seemed more dignified and tragic. It was an eerie bright night with the dark very clear outside of all the windows and Stella all rose-gold raging and crying around the room. Joel did not quite believe in picture actresses' grief. They have other preoccupations—they are beautiful rose-gold figures blown full of life by writers and directors, and after hours they sit around and talk in whispers and giggle innuendoes, and the ends of many adventures flow through them. (p. 180)

As if to confirm his suspicions, a short time later while Joel and Miles are discussing pictures, Stella comes "suddenly back into the conversation as if they'd never discussed her personal affairs" (p. 181). She is incensed because old Beltzer tried to change her husband's picture and stands "hovering protectively over Miles, her eyes flashing with indignation in his behalf" (p. 181). It is at this moment that "Joel realized that he was in love with her" (p. 181). What he does not seem to realize is that Stella is deeply in love with her husband and that she has been using Joel, once again, in an effort to rekindle Miles's love and affection. Her displays of grief and jealousy during the afternoon and evening were real, not playacting.

The third and final crazy Sunday brings the story into sharp thematic focus. But first there is a Saturday night prelude, which blends illusion and reality. "Self-conscious in his silk hat against the unemployment"—a reminder of the economic reality, the depression—Joel waits outside the Hollywood Theatre (p. 183). When Stella and her friends arrive in their smart limousines, he learns that Miles has flown east for the Notre Dame football game after all. During the performance of the play, Joel "turned and looked at [Stella] and she looked back at him, smiling and meeting his eyes for as long as he wanted" (p. 184). Between acts, she suggests that afterwards they go to her house and "'talk.'" She expresses doubt that her husband has actually gone to South Bend, suspects that the telegram from there is not authentic. "'Supposing he was here watching everything I do,'" she wonders (p. 184). Later, after saying goodnight to the others, they drive along a boulevard under a full moon which is "only a prop." "'If Miles had trained a camera on them," an angry Joel thinks, "he felt no obligations toward Miles" (p. 185). When they arrive at the house, Stella finds another telegram, this one from Chicago. "'You see,' she said, throwing the slip back on the table, 'he could easily have faked that'" (p. 185).

Joel now suspects that he is being used as a "'pawn in a spite game'" that Stella is playing against her husband (p. 186). A remark by Miles earlier in the week apparently planted the seed of suspicion: "'I can't tell what Stella might do just out of spite,'" he said (p. 182). Joel vaguely senses that he is caught up in a struggle between rival ingenuities, but when confronted, Stella refuses to confirm or to deny it. Evasively, she offers him a drink instead. Undeterred, Joel declares his "love," then spends the next half hour trying to seduce her. (One recalls that Joel had posed as a man of honor just a few days before. "'I've never made any passes whatsoever at Stella,'" he told Miles on Wednesday. "' . . . You can trust me absolutely'" [p. 182].) When she rebuffs him, he feels "faintly relieved" that an entanglement has been avoided (p. 186), a curious response for a rejected lover. Actually he is not in love with Stella Calman, the attractive wife and mother; rather he is fascinated by Stella Walker, the beautiful rose-gold actress blown full of life by his imagination. As usual, he is having difficulty in separating his true emotions from the false. As he prepares to take his leave, somewhat hurt by Stella's readiness to have him go, the phone rings—and the clock strikes.

Twelve o'clock ushers in another crazy Sunday and signals, for the reader at least, a return to reality. The voice on the phone reads from a telegram reporting a plane crash west of Kansas City. Miles Calman is dead, and Stella Calman desperately needs someone to lean on in her hour of need. Stella, however, refuses to believe the first, and Joel is unable to recognize the reality of the second. She pleads with him to stay and not to call anyone; frantically, she is trying to deny the reality of her husband's death by sustaining the *illusion* of a romantic triangle. She is not a cheap tramp trying to lure him to her bed. She is "'frightened'" and "'alone'" (pp. 187, 188). Even when others start to arrive, when the door-bell begins to ring and automobiles are pulling up in front of the door, she begs him to stay. Now she really needs the affection and friendship which she earlier exploited to make her husband jealous. She is still the beautiful golden girl, despite the death of the man whose "magical" touch had made her a screen star. Hers is a natural beauty which is not dependent on hair dyes, or facial make-up, or camera angles, or talented directors. Beautifully gowned as ever, she stands before Joel, but he sees only a ragged little gamin. His perception of "reality" leads Joel right back into the illusory world of the fairy tale—and the film studio: the director has left the set, but the actress, refusing to acknowledge that the scene is over, continues to emote on the empty stage. Joel has never quite believed in actresses' grief, and now when a lovely young woman appeals to him from the depths of her loss and sorrow, he is not convinced that her need is real. Promising to come back "'if you need me'" (p. 189), he stalks off the "set" praising the man whom, only moments before, he fully intended to betray. He abandons the one person who, just two short weeks ago, stood by him in his hour of need when he was suffering through his drunken embarrassment and sober disgrace. Thus, once again, and on the very same stage, Joel plays the fool. On that ironic note, the story concludes.[12]

Fitzgerald once explained in an essay on his craft that if he were to avoid false starts he had to "start out with an emotion—one that's close to me and that I can understand."[13] Certainly, he had played the fool many times himself and had blurred, and sometimes crossed over, the line between illusion and reality. During his first Hollywood sojourn in 1927, for instance, one madcap night he "made the Hollywood skies literally rain down money in silver puddles." According to Aaron Latham, Scott obtained a hundred dollars in coins from the desk clerk; he then threw handfuls of silver up against the windows of the Ambassador Hotel, shouting, "'It's money, it's money, it's money! It's free!'"[14] Just four years later he returned to Hollywood to work in films because, as he admitted, "he needed the money badly."[15] Little wonder then that Fitzgerald would remark, "'Sometimes I don't know whether I'm real or whether I'm a character in one of my own novels.'"[16]Fitzgerald's special gift as a writer was his ability to perceive the reality behind the glittering carnival, the face behind the mask. But occasionally he must have wondered if the time would ever come when he would no longer be able to separate the real from the unreal, "to detect where the milk is watered and the sugar is sanded, the rhinestone passed for diamond and the stucco for stone."[17] Clearly, that day has arrived for Joel Coles in "Crazy Sunday." Although alcohol is a contributing factor, Joel's inability to distinguish between appearance and reality is primarily the result of having lived and worked too long in a world of make-believe. When he comes face to face with genuine, shattering grief, he fails to recognize or to respond to it. The situation is no more real to him than a scene from a film script or a page from a fairy tale.

Notes

1. F. Scott Fitzgerald, *The Crack-Up*, ed. Edmund Wilson (New York: New Directions, 1945), p. 180.

2. F. Scott Fitzgerald, "One Hundred False Starts," in *Afternoon of an Author*, ed. Arthur Mizener (New York: Charles Scribner's, 1957), p. 132.

3. F. Scott Fitzgerald, "Crazy Sunday," in *Taps at Reveille* (New York: Charles Scribner's, 1935), p. 189. All further references to "Crazy Sunday" are to page numbers in this edition, cited parenthetically in the text.

4. Matthew J. Bruccoli, ed., *As Ever, Scott Fitz-: Letters between F. Scott Fitzgerald and his Literary Agent Harold Ober 1919–1940* (New York: J. B. Lippincott, 1972), p. 181.

5. *Ibid.*, p. 189.

6. Andrew Turnbull, *Scott Fitzgerald* (New York: Charles Scribner's, 1962), p. 202. Arthur Mizener, *The Far Side of Paradise* (Boston: Houghton Mifflin, 1951), p. 94. Neither Turnbull nor Mizener discusses "Crazy Sunday" in any detail.

7. Dwight Taylor, "Scott Fitzgerald in Hollywood," *Harper's*, 218 (March 1959), 70.

8. Turnbull, *Scott Fitzgerald*, p. 203.

9. Henry Dan Piper, *F. Scott Fitzgerald: A Critical Portrait* (New York: Holt, Rinehart and Winston, 1965), pp. 167, 263.

10. Sergio Perosa, *The Art of F. Scott Fitzgerald*, trans. Charles Matz and Sergio Perosa (Ann Arbor: Univ. of Michigan, 1965), p. 99.

11. Malcolm Cowley, ed., *The Stories of F. Scott Fitzgerald* (New York: Charles Scribner's, 1951), p. xiv.

12. As Joel sees it, the role of Miles Calman is similar to that of the fairy godmother in *Cinderella*. Miles is present, in body or spirit, at all three crazy Sundays, and he is instrumental in bringing Joel and Stella together on all three occasions. His magic spell ends at the stroke of midnight. Like Joel, Miles is basically insecure and morally weak, and has trouble separating the real from the unreal. He suspects his loyal, loving wife, although he is the one who is unfaithful. Once he sent down to the casting agency for a man with a long beard because he had a desire to drink tea with such a person and spent the whole afternoon doing just that. "The fine instinct that moved swiftly and confidently on the set, muddled so weakly and helplessly through his personal life" (p. 182).

13. Fitzgerald, "One Hundred False Starts," in *Afternoon of an Author*, p. 132.

14. Aaron Latham, *Crazy Sundays: F. Scott Fitzgerald in Hollywood* (New York: Viking, 1971), pp. 51–52.

15. Taylor, "Scott Fitzgerald in Hollywood," p. 68.

16. Quoted in Malcolm Cowley, "Third Act and Epilogue," in *F. Scott Fitzgerald: A Collection of Critical Essays*, ed. Arthur Mizener (Englewood Cliffs, N. J.: Prentice-Hall, 1963), p. 65.

17. Fitzgerald, "Pasting it Together," in *The Crack-Up*, p. 82.

WILLIAM J. BRONDELL

Structural Metaphors in Fitzgerald's Short Fiction

In a letter to Harold Ober, his agent, F. Scott Fitzgerald distinguished between two types of short stories: those that are "conceived like novels, which require a special emotion, a special experience," and present "something new, not in form, but substance"; and those "pattern stories" in which stock characters behave in a typical fashion and achieve a predictable ending, thus fulfilling, rather than challenging the reader's expectations.[1] About this latter kind, Fitzgerald parenthetically remarked, "It'd be better for me if I could do pattern stories, but the pencil just goes dead on me."[2]

In the forty-odd years since the publication of his last magazine story, careful readers of Fitzgerald have noticed that, despite his disclaimer, his pencil had often "gone dead" on him; that the larger portion of his short fiction exhibits a small amount of innovation in either form or substance. Clearly he could "do pattern stories," and did. In the same letter he says, "I wish I could think of a line of stories like the Josephine or Basil ones which could go faster & pay $3000."[3] Two of the stories in the Basil and Josephine series, "The Freshest Boy" and "A Nice Quiet Place," along with twelve more of his short stories, are noted as much for form as for their substance; all are ostensibly structured according to a conventional Five-Act dramatic model.[4] They generally reflect the time-honored Freytag structural pattern of Exposition, Rising Action, Crisis or Climax, Falling Action, and Resolution or

From *Kansas Quarterly* 14, no. 2 (Spring 1982): 95–112. Copyright © 1982 by *Kansas Quarterly*.

Denouement; but they are much freer in movement and not bound to a strict correspondence between their sections and the Freytag divisions. Fitzgerald usually spends a great deal more time and a greater number of sections on the rising action of his storms, often waiting until late in the fourth or fifth section before bringing the conflict to a climax. After that critical moment, when either the hero's fortunes or personality changes directions, the story races through the falling action and denouement.

In most of these stories, the hero or heroine reaches a psychological or moral nadir, or discovers a significant truth near the end of the fourth section. The last section then commonly resolves the plot by the use of a *deus ex machina*, a surprise, a trick reversal, or a further ironic discovery. Yet, although most of the plots, and the structures that advance the plots, seem contrived and artificial, nearly all of them exhibit a kind of logic or an appropriate motivation. Seldom does the protagonist step too far beyond the limits of probability and perform an action or say a word inappropriate to his or her character.

Judicious readers consign most of these five-act stories to a lower place in his canon; Fitzgerald himself recognized the weakness of five of them: " . . . Each story contains some special fault—sentimentality, faulty construction, confusing change of pace—or else was too obviously made for the trade."[5] Even though they inhabit the lower regions, Matthew Bruccoli gives them a fitting and reasoned epitaph: "Even his weak stories are redeemed by glimpses of what can be conveniently called 'the Fitzgerald touch'—wit, sharp observations, dazzling descriptions, or the felt emotion. . . . Above all, Fitzgerald's style shines through: the colors and rhythms of his prose."[6]

Three of the Five-Act stories "Absolution," "The Freshest Boy," and "Babylon Revisited," which on the surface follow the predictable and contrived pattern of the others, are another matter altogether. They exhibit that "special emotion" and "special experience" that characterize his best efforts in the novels, and they admirably realize Fitzgerald's "conception" in both form and substance.

From an examination of the major studies on Fitzgerald, and a careful reading of the relevant articles on his short fiction, several facts of Fitzgerald criticism emerge: (1) A great deal of critical attention has been paid to these three stories, though of the three, "Babylon Revisited" has engaged the most interest, "The Freshest Boy," the least; (2) Even though critics may have fundamentally irreconcilable opinions about the *real* meaning or significance of the stories, nearly all agree that there is much to praise and little to fault; (3) While most of the critical commentary addresses the issues of the "substance" and/or Fitzgerald's style, very little attention has been focused on the structure; (4) Those few commentators who discuss in more than a cursory fashion the structure of these stories have sometimes found (or invented) flaws, and thus have tempered their praise with a quiet reservation or two.

These reservations seem to be the result of a restricted analysis of the Five-Act structure: an insistence on tracing the flow of the action according to the conventional pattern. Undeniably, when their Five-Act structure is examined, these stories exhibit sufficient technical excellence to set them apart from their similarly patterned cousins. But in "Absolution," "The Freshest Boy," and "Babylon Revisited," Fitzgerald has not been content to use only the conventional form to control the movement of his "special experience" and "special emotion." In his best Five-Act stories, there are two discrete motions that flow along at their own pace and in their own direction yet in close harmony: an external movement of the central action; and an internal rhythm of the hero. To manage these motions, which support and fulfill each other, Fitzgerald has created two structures: a dramatic superstructure of five parts which develops the cause-and-effect relationships in the action; and a deep structure, whose phases vary from story to story, which traces the hero's psychological state as he responds to the action. The superstructure certifies the dramatic probability of the action; the deep structure verifies the psychological probability of the hero's response. In addition, just as Fitzgerald has indicated the pattern of the superstructure by dividing the movement of the action into five sections, he has suggested the pattern of the deep structure by providing a metaphor which informs the hero's psychological motion. In these three stories, the structural metaphor appears at a critical moment, just before the climax; and not only does it signal the impending crisis, it also resonates throughout the story's deep structure to motivate and to clarify the true nature of the crisis. Thus a close scrutiny of the structural metaphor and its implications might erase, or at least diminish, the reservations about the structure of the stories and, as a result, might bring into sharper focus the essential meaning of the story. At the very least, such an examination should give further support to the high praise these stories have received.

* * *

The superstructure created by Fitzgerald to carry the action of "Absolution" seems at first to deserve the criticism directed at it.[7] In his study of this short story John Higgins avers that despite the story's standing "among Fitzgerald's major achievement in the genre," the balance of the story is diminished somewhat by a major structural flaw: a "split character focus" in the story.[8] Such an opinion is logical if it grows out of a conviction that Rudolph is more than a general prototype of Gatsby—that he *becomes* Jimmy Gatz and then Jay Gatsby himself.[9] If this view of the necessary connection between

"Absolution" and *The Great Gatsby* controls an analysis of the structure, then Father Schwartz, who *must* be the antagonist in the conflict, receives too much attention. As a result, the importance of Rudolph's role as the protagonist is lessened. Undeniably, the framing sections set in the priest's rectory do focus on Schwartz, and the remainder of the plot does focus on Rudolph. With his eye on the *coda* that closes the story, Higgins concludes, "The last paragraph, which describes the sensuous Swede girls and echoes the opening scene, diverts the reader's attention from Rudolph to the priest."[10] Therefore the story is flawed in its structure. A careful examination of the structural metaphor of "Absolution" suggests that indeed there is a shift in focus, but that shift is not a flaw nor a weakness but a virtue and a strength.

The structural metaphor in "Absolution" appears in the Latin phrase which serves as a headnote to Section V: "*Sagitta Volante in Dei.*"[11] Fitzgerald excerpted the phrase from Psalm 90 in the Vulgate, and in the process, metastasized the last word of the phrase from "*die*" to "*Dei.*" There is no certain way of knowing whether the metathesis was deliberate or accidental, for all of the extant versions of the story exhibit the same transformation.[12] From what is known of Fitzgerald's casual attention to the rules of spelling, and especially his habit of writing "etc." as "ect.," it seems reasonable to assume that the error was accidental. If the assumption is correct, then the phrase should be translated, "Arrows flying by day," rather than "Arrows flying to God."[13] Moreover, some twenty years after the composition of "Absolution" Fitzgerald repeats the phrase, correctly, in "Sleeping and Waking": "*Scuto circumdabit te veritas eius; non timebis a timore nocturno, a sagitta volante in die, a negotio perambulante in tenebris*" ("His faith will surround you as a shield; you will not fear the terror of the night, nor the arrows flying by day, nor the trouble moving about in the darkness").[14] The extended quotation from the essay suggests that Fitzgerald knew the Psalm in its entirety, and selected the middle verses to fit his particular needs at the time of composition. In "Sleeping and Waking" the quotation is used to describe a "sinister, ever widening interval" between the "first sweet sleep of night," and the last deep sleep of the morning.[15]

The headnote then seems to apply immediately to Father Schwartz: of all the characters in the story, he is the most likely to know the phrase. Psalm 90 frequently appears in the breviary from which, according to ecclesiastical law, he must read daily, and it has a prominent place in the Compline service for Sundays. Moreover, the "sinister" and fearful aspects of the quotation are reflected in both the first and last sections of the story, where the priest, a depressed and frightened creature, is brought to the edge of madness by the assault of the "heat and sweat and life" of the world.

In Section I Father Schwartz's senses are under continuing attack by the world outside his rectory windows. He hears the "shrill laughter" of the

Swedish girls; he sees the "yellow lights" and "gleaming" nickel taps in the drugstore; he smells the sweet "cheap toilet soap" that floats upward "like incense toward the summer moon." Under such a constant barrage of the noises and smells and sights of the daylight world, he tries to escape: often by a prayer for darkness to come to quiet the laughter; sometimes, when he is caught out in the open between the church and his rectory, by a detour around the lights and the smell of soap emanating from the drugstore. But there is no escape; he is trapped in his room with the world outside full of heat and life and terror. Even his thoughts are imprisoned in "grotesque labyrinths" from which there is no escape from "the unavoidable sun." By the end of the first two paragraphs of the story, Father Schwartz has "reached the point where the mind runs down like an old clock."

When he comes into focus again in Section V, the priest's depressive condition seems not to have undergone any great obvious change during Rudolph's confession. The same "cold watery eyes" are fixed upon the same carpet pattern of lifeless figures of "flat bloomless vines and the pale echoes of flowers"—echoing, ironically, the outside world with its ripening and wind-blown wheat, golden in the afternoon sun. Yet he seems to be in the manic phase of his psychosis, for he begins to hallucinate and to watch his rosary beads change into evil snakes and crawl about on the green felt of his table. He struggles out of his hallucination and startles Rudolph with a peculiar non-sequitur that in some ways is an image of the Communion of Saints: "When a lot of people get together in the best places things go glimmering." The priest then describes for the boy the distinction between the world as it is, full of life and activity, and the world as he wishes it to be. "Do you hear the hammer and the clock ticking and the bees? Well, that's no good. The thing is to have a lot of people in the centre of the world, wherever that happens to be."

Later in the fifth section, with his eyes "dried out and hot," signifying an increasingly desperate deterioration in his condition, Father Schwartz envisions a seductive yet pernicious world. It is an amusement park filled with the sights, sounds, and smells of life. He says, "You'll see a big wheel made of lights turning in the air. . . ." There will be the sounds of a "band playing somewhere," and the "smell of peanuts." But the priest warns Rudolph, "Don't get up close, because if you do you'll only feel the heat and the sweat and the life." This admonition has already been given to Rudolph in another form during the boy's first confession in Section II: "Don't you know, my child, that you should avoid the occasions of sin as well as the sin itself?" There can be no clearer statement of the priest's fear of life than this. To him, all the world is an occasion of sin. Thus, in his scrupulous and fearful world, the laughter of the Swedish girls, and the gleaming nickel taps of the soda fountain, and the sweet incense of the soap are the "arrows flying by day" into the very heart of Father Schwartz. The Ferris wheel and the band and the peanuts become the "terrors of the night."[16]

Certainly there are enough associations between Father Schwartz and the headnote to clarify his psychological state; but the metaphor can also be seen as an index of Rudolph's interior life. Not that the boy is another example of the fear of life, for his personality and actions described in the early sections put him in direct conflict with the priest. But even though the two are in conflict and, on some levels, obvious foils for each other, by the end of Section IV they have come into a condition of psychological and spiritual parity.

The fundamental nature of this parity is only suggested in Section I. Father Schwartz's state of depression and the fears that have caused it are already at a critical stage before Rudolph is ushered into the room. They are immediately locked together by their eyes; the priest, with his "cold watery eyes," stares into Rudolph's "enormous, staccato eyes, lit with gleaming points of cobalt light." The contrast is as obvious as the connection. The two disparate characters are more firmly joined when the priest, on the margin of a breakdown from his terrors, sees that the boy is in a similar "state of abject fear." Rudolph intimates the cause of his fear when he confesses "in a despairing whisper" that he has committed a "terrible sin": a sin worse than impurity, worse than murder. Despite their obvious differences in age, experience, and knowledge; despite the symbolic contrast between the gloomy Father Schwartz, whose very name in German means "darkness," and the beautiful boy who sits in the patch of sunlight, the two protagonists of the story converge on several levels. The priest is afraid of life; and Rudolph is fearful of the consequences of his undescribed "terrible sin"; the priest is isolated from God, unable to achieve a "mystical union with our Lord"; and the boy in his sinning has turned away from God. Yet, although they converge in this section, they have not merged in their parity. The priest's psychological and spiritual state is almost terminal, whereas the state of Rudolph's soul is only implied. It is the function of the middle sections to fulfill the implications.

The middle flashback sections (II–IV), wherein Rudolph comes into prime focus, describe his inevitable fall from a state of grace to mortal sin. The central action of each section is Rudolph's proud and sinful rebellion against a figure of authority, against a father. The rebellion always takes place in the home of the particular father against whom Rudolph rebels, and it is always followed by an imaginative attempt to escape, not the guilt, but the consequences of the rebellion. These escape attempts, and the fear that prompts them, lead inexorably to another graver sinful act. The moral tangle continues until Rudolph commits a sacrilegious communion near the end of Section IV.

The middle sections also trace the development of Rudolph's responses to his moral condition. Rudolph's first sin, which initiates his fall, is really not a serious sin. Two of the necessary requirements for grave sin are absent: sufficient reflection, and the will to do wrong. In fact, "something almost exterior to himself dictated" the lie. Later in the second section Rudolph himself has trouble defining the gravity of his sin. He describes it once as a "terrible sin," then a "bad mistake." Still later he feels the "horrors of his lie," but diminishes that description a few lines later when he "considered how he could best avoid the consequences of his misstatement." Rudolph's psychological state and his reactions to the lie match his inability to define accurately the gravity of his sin.

Before his confession, as he waits outside the confessional, the "large coffin set on end," his spirits are low: "Fear assumed solid form and pressed out a lodging between his heart and his lungs." Shortly after his lie he feels like "the commoner in the king's chair"; still later he escapes his fear by becoming his alter ego, Blatchford Sarnemington. Eventually, his "exhilaration faded out and his mind cooled, and he felt the horror of his lie." Clearly Rudolph's fears are no greater after his lie than they were before. They certainly are not to a stage of equality with the priest's fears. Rudolph's lies in Section III are defensive evasions and venial in nature. In respect to his psychological responses to his actions, he is more afraid of a possible beating by his father than he is of a "thunderbolt" from God. But in Section IV, his moral state and his psychological condition grow critical. Forced to attend confession again, he lies to spite his father, and in so doing steps a bit deeper into sin. His initial response is one of "maudlin exultation." But as the time to take communion approaches, he feels that "there was no reason why God should not stop his heart." The next paragraph shows his growing fear not only of death, but of death by execution. As he kneels at the communion rail waiting for the host, "a cold sweat broke out on his forehead ... and with gathering nausea Rudolph felt his heart valves weakening." Just before he receives the host, he bows his head, not in adoration but in fearful expectation of the worst; and in that position, he "waited for the blow." The last image of Section IV suggests the completeness of Rudolph's isolation from God, and from everyone else. As the other communicants leave the communion rail they are "alone with God." But Rudolph "was alone with himself, drenched with perspiration and deep in mortal sin." In that state he feels like a fallen angel walking back to his pew on his "cloven hoofs."

The nature of his "terrible sin" and his "abject fear" is now certain. His fears and his spiritual condition are now on a par with Father Schwartz's. The two troubled souls, priest and boy, Father and son, are brought together by their fears. The Father fears life and the boy fears death. Both seek help and protection from each other; both require absolution. At the moment of the climax their association is more of a sterile symbiosis, wherein two dissimilar souls feed off each other, yet derive little spiritual benefit from their union. It is Rudolph's eyes like "blue stones" and lashes that spray out "like flower petals" that remind the priest of the arrows that fly by day and push him into his spiral toward unconsciousness; it is the priest's mad visions and his subsequent collapse that send Rudolph fleeing from the Church. They have come together seeking forgiveness, but have been denied.

Despite this convergence, which fulfills the implications of the structural metaphor, their fears are not sufficient motivation for the action that follows. The essential action of the climax to which these kindred souls have been brought concerns the necessary elements in the Sacrament of Penance: confession, contrition, absolution—and a sin. But clearly, fear is not a sin. Father Schwartz's avoidance of the "heat and sweat" of life is not *sui generis* a sinful act. And even though his imagination has turned him into a devil, Rudolph has confessed his lies and sacrileges to the priest, and has even calmed down. Thus it is not fear that causes their exchange of roles and eventual separation; it is their sin. The headnote suggests the nature of their sin: they both exhibit signs of an imperfect faith; one which denies the dual nature of Christ.

The essential thrust of Psalm 90 is that the man who trusts in God, who "*habitat in adjutorio Altissimus*" ("he dwells in the shelter of the Almighty"), will receive several benefits as a result of his faith.[17] These benefits, suggested in a series of metaphors in the first thirteen verses of the Psalm, promise protection, defense, and refuge from all the world's enmity. In the last three verses, God himself speaks and promises to protect, deliver and glorify the believer: "*Quoniam in me speravit, liberabo eum; protegam eum, quoniam cognovit me*" ("Because he has hoped in me, I will free him; I will protect him, because he has known my name"). Of special significance to the climax of "Absolution" is God's vow, "*Clamabit ad me, et ego exaudiam eum; cum ipso sum in tribulatione*" ("He calls out to me, and I will hear him; I will be with him in his tribulation").

By the end of the first paragraph of Section V, it is clear that Rudolph has called upon the Lord. He has confessed his sin, and has grown less fearful; he even feels a sense of security in "God's shelter" because the representative of God is with him: "He knew that as long as he was in the room with this priest God would not stop his heart." As it turns out, this faith is imperfect, for God's representative is too much concerned with his own problems to help Rudolph. At the end of the story, Rudolph is left alone with only his imagination as a refuge against the spiritual death he fears, and he runs "in panic" away from the rectory, the bogus shelter of God.

Father Schwartz also calls upon the Lord in Section V. Soon after his vision of the amusement park, and after the "horror" of his realization "entered suddenly at the open window," the priest "collapsed precipitously down on his knees." In at least the position, if not the attitude of prayer and supplication, he cries out, "Oh my God!" This may be a cry of despair; but it could also be a call for help. His words are identical to the first three words of the *Confiteor*; and they are the same words that Basil recited "meaninglessly" after his first confession. Like Rudolph's, his act of contrition, his call to the Lord in time of grave peril, may very well not be answered—it may be voiced too late in a life characterized by an imperfect faith.

Earlier, in an attempt to "fix" Rudolph's guilt and absolve him, Father Schwartz says, "Apostasy implies an absolute damnation only on the supposition of a previous perfect faith." Undeniably, the critical problem in the spiritual lives of both protagonists is that neither one can be supposed to have a perfect faith. The two fundamental dogmas of the Catholic faith which both profess are the Trinity, which proves the divinity of Christ, and the Incarnation, which accomplishes His humanity. As Aquinas states, *"Duo nobis credenda proponuntur: occultum Divinitas ... et mysterium humanitatis Christi"* ("Two things are proposed for believing: the secret of the Divinity and the mystery of the humanity of Christ").[18] Instead of dwelling in the shelter of the Almighty, and of believing in His mercy and His humanity, Father Schwartz has retreated to his dark and dingy room, crossed the street to avoid the sweet smells, and turned his eyes away from the sights of a world filled with warmth and love. In emphasizing the justice and vengeance of God the Father because of his fear, he has denied the mercy and humanity of the Son of God, the Christ he has vowed to serve.

Rudolph, whose instruction in the faith of his fathers has been in the hands of Father Schwartz, exhibits the same kind of exaggerated insistence on the vengeance of God. It is clear throughout the scenes dealing with his confessions and his sins that he has misunderstood the true nature of the Sacrament of Penance and the real meaning of Absolution. In Section V, after he hears the priest's description of the amusement park, he mistakenly feels that "there was something ineffably gorgeous somewhere that had nothing to do with God." In essence, he has denied the omnipresence of God, and thus in a sense, the divinity of God. Obviously, Father Schwartz has failed twice to give Rudolph the proper instruction in the faith; he has not fulfilled his duty as a pastor, to lead men to a perfect faith.

Thus the deep structure informed by the headnote has carried two protagonists to an unbearably tense moment in their spiritual and psychological development. Their imperfect faith cannot protect them from each other nor from the debilitating effects of their fears. They can only call out to the wrong God, as does Rudolph, or call out too late, as does Father Schwartz. The ultimate condition of their souls is not certain, but is certainly suggested in the story's last paragraph.

The coda implies in its imagery the futility and waste in a life controlled by an imperfect faith. The crisis in faith of both heroes, identical in design and equal in psychological intensity, has arrived at the turning point in the confinement of the priest's room: a dingy, haunted, stale and lifeless box. But outside, the "hot fertile life" goes on as indifferent to the fearful world of Father Schwartz as it is to the imaginative, almost Byronic world of Rudolph. In its warmth and life, and in its fluid and natural movement, the coda is a remarkable comment on the constricted and barren scene of two souls who, because of the imperfect faith, failed to find the refuge and comfort they sought.

*   *   *

The chief reservation about the structural excellence of "The Freshest Boy" grows out of considerations of the last section of the story. Kenneth Eble calls the ending of the story "overly dramatic"; and John Higgins, following Eble's lead, claims that "the redemption scene is weak in motivation and hence in plausibility."[19] A brief examination of the superstructure will mitigate the impact of Higgins's statement; and an analysis of the structural metaphor will show that the ending of the story *is* out of proportion with the rest of the story, because the romantic personality of Basil Lee naturally tends to the "overly dramatic."

Unlike "Absolution," "The Freshest Boy" moves easily and naturally through its Five-Act superstructure. The introductory section, or the exposition, clearly indicates the protagonist, his special romantic personality, and his impending conflicts. Sections II and III move the protagonist down the vortex of unpopularity and isolation until at the end of Section III, he is alone in his room, rejected by his school masters and classmates, and in the deepest despondency of his young life. The climactic Section IV traces his journey to New York, where he considers fleeing his difficulties at St. Regis school, and then moves to his epiphany wherein he discovers an important truth about life and gets "wise" to himself. After his discovery Basil decides against flight and makes his first unselfish motion toward another human being. Section V, the denouement, quickly describes his attempts to act according to his new-found wisdom, and ends with a reward for his endeavors. There are no hitches, no breaks, and no delays in Basil's fall and rise. There is a clear line of motivation and a careful and trenchant system of correspondences that result in a tight unity in the superstructure. This unity can be seen in Section IV as Fitzgerald develops an ironic analogy between the world of romantic illusions and reality.

In this climactic section, Basil really attends two three-act plays: the romantic musical comedy, "The Quaker Girl," which traces the separation and reunion of two lovers; and the real-life drama which describes the union and separation of Ted Fay and his love, the heroine of "The Quaker Girl."[20]

Act I of the musical comedy is set in "The Village Green of a Small Town near New York," and the action it portrays, as seen through the eyes of Basil, is the tragic separation of two lovers who have had a misunderstanding: "The girl—the man. What kept them apart even now? Oh, these tragic errors and misconceptions. So sad." During the first intermission, Basil sees Ted Fay "leaning rather moodily" against a back wall of the theater. The equations between the comedy and the drama that is to follow are as clear as they are appropriate. Ted Fay, Basil's idol, the star football player from Yale, is the "man." New Haven is the "small village near New York"; Fay's lover, Jerry, plays the role of the heroine in the play. As can be inferred from the later conversation that Basil overhears, Fay and Jerry have fallen in love (perhaps when the play tried out in New Haven), and their relationship has arrived at a critical point just as "The Quaker Girl" opens, with Jerry on stage and a "rather moody" Ted Fay in the audience with Basil.

In Act II, the action moves to "The Foyer of the Hotel Astor" where the heroine, "carried away by the glitter of it all," becomes the "toast of the shining town." After half an hour, she scorns her lover by throwing his gift of roses at his feet, and turning and dancing with another. As the act draws to a close, the heroine's theme song, "Beautiful Rose of the Night," is heard again. In the corresponding real-life drama, Fay and the heroine have moved to the tea room of the Knickerbocker Hotel, where Jerry rejects Fay's gift of himself, choosing instead to take a different partner, Beltzman, the producer of her play.

Act III, which takes place on "The Roof Garden of Mr. Van Astor's House," brings the musical comedy to a close with a predictably happy ending. Although Basil doesn't dwell on specific details, he sees that "Everything was going to be all right, after all." There is a "promise of felicity" and a "lovely plaintive duet," probably sung by the reunited lovers, then the "long moment of incomparable beauty" is over. The conclusion to Ted and Jerry's "play" is less happy. As Basil, an audience of one, sits quietly near their table in the tea room, he overhears Jerry's plan to marry her producer, and the truth that changes both Ted Fay's and his own life: "This isn't a musical comedy, Ted." Instead of singing a "lovely duet" to celebrate their reunion, they say goodbye. Ted Fay will go back to New Haven, and Jerry will continue her career. Instead of the "promise of felicity" there will be only the memory of that afternoon. Basil leaves the concluding act of this drama in a state of "wild emotional confusion," for he has learned a significant truth about the difference between the real world and the world of illusion: "Life for everybody was a struggle, sometimes magnificent from a distance, but always and surprisingly simple and a little sad."

Basil has traveled to New York and the theater to escape from his miserable existence at St. Regis; but he has witnessed a sad drama from real life that prompts him to return to school. Like his idol, who will carry the memory of this day with him as he returns to Yale to continue his life, Basil will go back to his school to continue his struggle. When the struggles and failures described in Section V become too great, he will draw sustenance from his New York experience: "There was Ted Fay, and 'Rose of the Night' on the phonograph—'all my life whenever I hear that waltz'—and the remembered lights of New York." Clearly, Fitzgerald's use of the play as a metaphor for the climax of the story fulfills the expectations of the first three sections and leads inevitably, in a tight motivational chain, to the "redemption" scene. In addition, he employs "The Quaker Girl" and Basil's response to the play as a metaphor for the deep structure of the story. Under the influence of the metaphor, the deep structure of the story is now divided into three acts which are analogous to the typical musical comedy structure. Section I becomes the overture, or program; Sections II and III are the rising action as in Act I of the play; Section IV becomes Act II; and the final section is an analogue to Act III.

Fitzgerald states immediately prior to Act I of the cited comedy that the "program itself had a curious sacredness—a prototype of the thing itself." As the program is the prototype of the play, the play is an ironic prototype of the Ted Fay–Jerry relationship. And the play can also be seen as a prototype of the story. In a sense, as Basil discovers the truth about life after watching the two three-act plays, the reader discovers the truth about Basil, after watching him move through the three acts of his life at St. Regis.

Somewhat like an overture, which provides a preview of the major songs to be heard later in the play, and even more like a program that lists the cast and generally describes the structure of the play, the expository section foreshadows the significant action of the story to follow. It is a self-contained unit of three interrelated movements: it begins with a daydream and ends with a daydream; sandwiched in between the two dreams is a real-world struggle between two young boys, opposite in character, feelings, and knowledge. The first dream characterizes Basil's romantic hopes; the interlude suggests the problem that dashes these hopes; and the final dream of athletic glory foreshadows Basil's victory over his problems.

The action of the first daydream takes place in a Broadway restaurant filled with a "brilliant and mysterious group of society people," especially a girl with "dark hair and dark tragic eyes" who wears French perfume. In the guise of the mysterious Shadow, Basil enters the room with gun in hand, glances around, announces his identity, and, "like a flash, turns and goes into the night." Basil's dream then dissolves into the reality of Lewis Crum, Basil's companion on the train ride to St. Regis. It is Lewis who establishes the central conflict of the story, the struggle between Basil's "freshness" and the rest of the boarding school world. After some argument started over Basil's boast of playing football for St. Regis, Lewis prophesies, "You wait! They'll take all that freshness out of you." Basil escapes from Lewis's "dismal presence" by reentering the dream world. However, the setting for this final dream of Act I is the playing field at St. Regis. Basil is called from the bench with two minutes to play and his team down by three points. "Lee!" his coach calls, "It all depends on you now." As his signal is called by the quarterback, Basil awakens, and, anxious for the glory he is sure to come, he says, "I wish we'd get there before tomorrow." All three of these episodes, the two dreams and the real world interlude, will reappear in an altered, significant, but ironic form in the action that follows.

The setting and actions and characters of the first act of "The Quaker Girl" now begin to reverberate through Sections II and III of the story. There is no more appropriate setting for the "freshest boy" from the Midwest than a "village green," especially when his ignorance of the ways of boarding school, and his annoying personality are so aptly portrayed in Section II. He is as unsophisticated as the Quaker girl must have been. Moreover, the St. Regis campus is located near East Chester, a small "suburban farming community" near New York. The principal action and tone of the play also mirror the incidents in the story and Basil's response to them. The misunderstandings, the "tragic errors," the separation, and the sadness all have their counterpart in the story.

Section II is a long and realistic description of Basil's difficulties at school and his descent into loneliness. As he searches for companions to travel with him to New York, he meets rejection at every turn. He is first spurned by Bugs Brown, a "typical lunatic." Then Fat Gaspar, a boy of prodigal pleasantness and indiscriminate affection, refuses "indifferently." Finally, Treadway, Basil's roommate of only a week and thus innocent of Basil's personality and "humiliations," prefers to "cut their friendly relations short," and to reject him. Thus the crazy, the kind-hearted, and the ignorant all separate from Basil. The prophecy of Lewis Crum, whose "dismal but triumphant voice" has the last word, is now fulfilled. The theme struck in the second movement of the "overture" section is heard again.

The separation and sadness of the play's first act are reflected in an even more melodramatic fashion in Section III. Unable to find even one student to accompany him, Basil returns disconsolately to his room. He spends his time trying to choose his favorite pin-up from a package of eight Harrison Fisher photographs. After some listless deliberation, his eyes are finally drawn to "Babette, a dark little violet-eyed beauty," who seems more romantic and mysterious than all the others. While Basil sobs into his pillow, and flails away at those who have rejected him, Treadway enters the room and begins to pack his belongings. When questioned, Treadway announces, "I'm moving in with Wales," takes a last look about the room's "new barrenness," and leaves. This last blow, the loss of his roommate to his arch enemy, evokes a mournful, "Poor little Babette! Poor little Babette!" All alone at the nadir of his life, he seeks the comfort and companionship of a glossy reproduction of a coquettish French girl, whose eyes and hair and romantic nature are remarkably like the dark-haired girl of the opening daydream. The high spirits and romantic hopes embodied in the first section are now in ruins at the end of the third.

Act II of the musical comedy continues to be an analogue of Basil's life in Section IV. The heroine of the play has left the village and has come to New York, to the "Foyer of the Hotel Astor." She has become an overnight sensation, and because of her unsophisticated background, she is caught up in a kind of life style very different from and more exciting than her former way of life. Entranced by her new life and her stardom, she spurns her village lover, and "dances wildly" with her new lover. But at the end of the act, the romantic strains of her theme song, so "poignant and aching," signal a forthcoming change in the direction of her life as they catch her again "like a leaf helpless in the wind" and carry her into—Act III. Similarly, Basil has escaped the "dismal and dreary round of school," and traveled to New York. He also finds himself in the foyer, or on the threshold, of a new, liberating experience. His mother's letter affords him a real opportunity to escape from school and flee to Europe: "Almost strangling with happiness," he turns his back on school, crying out, "'No more St. Regis!'" Now Doctor Bacon and Mr. Rooney and Brick Wales and Fat Gaspar are only "impotent shadows in the stationary world that he was sliding away from, sliding past, waving his hand." But after his epiphany, wherein he loses his "freshness" and "gets wise" to himself, he realizes that he will not go to Europe, but will return to school—in Section V.

Basil now is in the final act of his life's story at St. Regis; and Act III of "The Quaker Girl" is an equivalent figure of that story. The program is now fulfilled: the heroine and her lover are quickly reunited on the roof garden (the city's echo of a village green); they sing "one lovely plaintive duet"; and only the passage of time is necessary to realize the "promise of felicity" in the anachronistic "bright tropical sky." In the corresponding last section of the story, Basil returns to school, armed with new knowledge and with a renewed commitment to his three-act dream of "the conquest of the successive worlds of school, college and New York." He makes "numberless new starts" and fails. But buoyed up by his recollections of the trip to New York, he survives the winter of his discontent. Eventually he is reunited with Fat Gaspar and the others; even the masters and the small boys who were first to move away from him now move closer. His new life at school has not been as felicitous as the musical promised, but one February afternoon, "a great thing happened"; which ironically recalls both Act III of the play and Section I of the story.

This "great thing" is nothing more than a "poor makeshift" of a nick-name bestowed on him by his enemy, Brick Wales. It is a "poor makeshift" because Wales is "unconscious that he had done anything in particular." But to Basil it is a signal of his acceptance and the proof that he is finally reunited with all of those from whom he has been separated. The calling out of his nickname, "Lee-y!" a name which "could scarcely be pronounced," is a far cry from a "lovely plaintive duet"; but it is better than "Bossy." The irony expands even further when the final dream of Section I is recalled. Before Basil's "play" begins, he dreams of being called ("Lee!") by his coach to rescue the varsity football team from defeat in the big game of the year. As his "comedy" comes to its conclusion, Basil is playing second-string basketball during a scrimmage and is called ("Lee-y!") by Brick Wales, who only wants the ball himself—and Basil makes a "poor pass." To a boy whose fictional life has moved in five sections, but whose romantic interior life has been divided according to the three acts of a musical comedy, Basil's response is indeed "overly dramatic," but eminently "plausible" and well-motivated. The motivation is further enhanced by a final correspondence. Basil takes his unpronounceable nickname "to bed with him that night," and holds it close "happily to the last" as he falls "easily to sleep." In the last scene of Section III he has also gone to bed with a name; but "Babette" was the name he had for comfort in his loneliest hours. Thus Sections I, III, and V are tied together: the imagined glory of I has yielded to the despair of III and has been ironically fulfilled in V.

In "The Freshest Boy," Fitzgerald has cleverly created two structures to describe Basil's progress through his first year of school: a superstructure which defines the external action of Basil's getting "wise to himself"; and a deeper structure which clarifies the boy's interior life—a life so moved by imagination and romance that Basil does not clearly "understand all he has heard." Basil's romantic response to the "poor makeshift" world of reality suggests that he has grown in knowledge, but not in wisdom. But of course, "The Freshest Boy" is only the first act in Basil's three-act comedy of "school, college and New York."

* * *

"Babylon Revisited" has deservedly received more critical attention and praise than any other Fitzgerald short story, with most commentators expressing admiration for its flawless blend of a tight, balanced structure and a significant theme. The only reservation about the story's structural excellence appears in a footnote to Higgins' study of the story: "The story's structure seems slightly flawed in that there are actually two dramatic climaxes, scene four and scene six."[21] One sees a flaw only if one insists on a restricted development in the superstructure; such an emphasis traditionally demands that the climax be followed by a change in the hero's fortunes or in his psychological state. There is obviously a change in Charlie's fortunes and psychological state after Marion relents and yields to Charlie's request for custody of Honoria. But then of course the story continues; and just as his desires are to be fulfilled, the "ghosts" out of the past intervene and turn Charlie into a victim instead of a victor—his fortunes change and his spirit falls. But clearly, Charlie's loneliness at the end of the story is appropriate only if he has been deprived of Honoria, as happened in the climax in Scene six, Section IV.

Even though some disagree with Seymour Gross's interpretation of the ultimate meaning of the story, his reading of "Babylon Revisited" remains the most judicious and detailed appraisal of the relationships between the structure and the theme—so detailed that the following examination of the deep structure and the structural metaphor will be but a fine-tuning of his argument and a moderation of his gloomy interpretation.[22] Gross notices, analyzes, and expands on the structural "maneuvers" Fitzgerald uses to achieve the unity and coherence that raises this story above the others. Since "Babylon Revisited" is essentially a story of Charlie's character, Gross correctly sees Charlie as having attained the fundamental state of a man of character, a "quiet power over himself."[23] But despite this self mastery, Charlie needs "his daughter back to give shape and direction to his renascence, to redeem his lost honor, and in a sense to recover something of his wife."[24] Charlie's failure to accomplish this "crushes any lingering hopes" that he might have had, and leaves him with nothing to do "but turn for comfort to the dead for whom time has also stopped."[25] Gross's attention is focused primarily on the superstructure and on the action moved along by the extensive parallels between the sections of that structure; as a result, he sees the story as a tightly woven yet simple description of a man cruelly and unjustly denied both his daughter and his honor. A brief analysis of the deep structure of Charlie's internal life and the special metaphor that informs the deep structure suggest that "Babylon Revisited" is indeed a story on two levels: the exterior level which describes Charlie's unsuccessful attempt to reclaim his daughter Honoria; and an interior level which describes Charlie's successful attempt to prove his reformation and thus reclaim his lost honor.

As in "The Freshest Boy," the structural metaphor in "Babylon Revisited," to be found immediately prior to the climax, informs both the superstructure and the deep structure. At the end of Section III, after Marion has agreed to relinquish her custody of Honoria, Charlie returns to his rooms in an "exultant" state of mind. But immediately, he discovers that he cannot sleep, because the "image of Helen haunted him." He begins to review their stormy relationship, and especially the particulars of the night when he, in a pique of jealous anger, locked her out in the snow. He then recalls the aftermath and all its horrors, the superficial "reconciliation," and the eventual death of his wife—"martyrdom," as Marion would have it. The memories are so strong and become so real that Charlie imagines that Helen talks to him. She reassures him that she also wants him to have custody of Honoria, and she praises him for his reformation. Then she says a "lot of other things— friendly things—but she was in a swing in a white dress, and swinging faster and faster all the time, so that at the end he could not hear clearly all that she said."[26] This image of Helen in the swing emanates throughout the story's superstructure. Just as the dream of his dead wife in a white dress (suggestive of the innocent past of long ago) swings into his mind to restrain his "exultation," so the sins of the past, in the shape and form of Lorraine and Duncan, will appear in Section IV to dash his hopes for the custody of Honoria. Similarly, the action of the swing reflects the pacing of the action in the climactic section: its faster and faster movement implies the quick arrival and departure of Lorraine and Duncan, Marion's abrupt change of heart, and the sudden reversal of Charlie's fortunes.

The metaphor with its back and forth motion not only serves to describe and motivate the climax, but also marks the progress of the action which precedes and follows the climax. From the beginning to the end, the plot is characterized by a series of alternating currents from the past to the present. Higgins has suggested that there are three interwoven movements in the story: "A continual reciprocating movement between his old and new world" in a series of seven scenes; "an in-and-out movement among past, present and future"; and the movement of Charlie's "emotional alternations between optimism and pessimism, hope and disillusion."[27] Clearly, every contact with the past seems to dampen Charlie's spirits or to cloud his expectations, or to defeat his hopes. Just as clearly, the swing functions as a metaphor of the intrusion of the past and reinforces the theme of man's inability to escape the consequences of his past behavior. Furthermore, because of its insistent continual motion, the metaphor seems to suggest that as long as Charlie's life continues, he will, like Sisyphus, almost reach the moment of joy; but something out of the past will turn him away. As Thomas Staley has remarked, "Time and its ravages have left Charlie suspended in time with a nightmare for a past, an empty whiskey glass for a present, and a future full of loneliness."[28] Or so it seems if only one level of action is examined. But as Gross has suggested, Charlie's attempt to reclaim his daughter implies an attempt to reclaim his lost honor; and the swing metaphor mirrors Charlie's efforts on this level.

According to the physics of swinging, there is a state of near-equivalence between the terminus of the forward motion and the terminus of the rearward motion. But if the swing must rely on its own momentum, the laws of gravity demand that the terminus of the succeeding motion be lower than the terminus of the preceding motion. There is a similar "balance" in the heights and depths of Charlie's emotional responses to the actions that elicit these responses. In a sense, the physical laws that control the swing are transformed into the metaphysical and ethical laws that govern Charlie's feelings. Thus for every action in the plot, there is Charlie's less-than-equal reaction—and never any overreaction. Unlike the reactions of every other character in the story, Charlie's are always under control. He may not be able to control the events of his life, but he can and does control his reactions. As he states in Section III while justifying his daily drink, "It's a sort of stunt I set myself. It keeps the matter in proportion."

Throughout the difficult inquisition in Section III, Charlie consciously restrains his natural desires to match the venom of Marion's accusations. "Keep your temper," he tells himself after discovering that he "would take a beating." When Marion recalls the morning after he had locked his wife out in the snow, Charlie "wanted to launch out into a long expostulation," but he doesn't. Later, he becomes "increasingly alarmed" because he feared for Honoria if she remained in the "atmosphere" of Marion's hostility. But "he pulled his temper down out of his face and shut it up inside him. . . ." Near the end of Section III, Marion, eaten up by her prejudice against him and her inescapable memories of her sister's death, cries out, "How much you were responsible for Helen's death I don't know." Even in this desperate moment, as he feels a "current of agony" surge through him, he "hung on to himself" and restrained his emotions—he kept "the matter in proportion." Even Marion realizes the extent of his mastery over himself: "She saw him plainly and she knew he had somehow arrived at control over the situation." In essence, by restraining his reactions, Charlie makes Marion's actions seem all the more out of control. Thus, by being more controlled and reasonable, Charlie proves his reformation and achieves a victory over Marion. For every swing of Marion's argument, Charlie swings back with a controlled response.

In the climactic fourth section the swing begins to move faster and faster, and Charlie's interior world moves in the same rhythm. The first paragraph clearly suggests this motion: "He made plans, vistas, futures for Honoria and himself, but suddenly he grew sad. . . ." In the next breath, he says, "The present was the thing; work to do and someone to love"; and then, "But not to love too much." His mind is swinging back and forth in rapid succession: the hopes for the future are controlled by his thoughts of the past; the sadness of the past is restrained by the needs of the present; and over all, a sense of control, of moderation.

It is this moderation and control that characterizes Charlie's response to the devastating swing of the past that squashes his hopes for reunion with Honoria. The climax brings into clear focus the essential nature of his "character," and his mastery over his emotions. After Lorraine and Duncan materialize, Charlie's attempts to control the situation prove fruitless. At first he was "astounded," then "anxious and at a loss." Later he approaches them "as if to force them backward down the corridor," back into the past.[29] But the momentum of their untimely visit can't be stopped; and in their swinging, they figuratively knock him out of the way: Marion changes her mind and therefore Charlie's future. His last lines in the section show the completeness of his self-control. They are peculiarly measured and restrained, not at all the farewell speech of a man who feels that he has lost everything he has ever wanted. His farewell to his daughter, "Good night, sweetheart," echoes Horatio's farewell to Hamlet; but Charlie broadens his farewell in order to lessen the possible tragic overtones: "Trying to make his voice more tender, trying to conciliate something, 'Good night, dear children.'" Undeniably, the action of the climax proves that even a man of strong character cannot control the actions and feelings of others, nor the strange, almost accidental swing of fortune; but, Charlie's reactions prove that a man who has mastery over his emotions and can control himself has a sense of integrity and honor that cannot be made hostage to the quirks of fate and the meanness of others.

In the first three sections of the story, Charlie's tactics of control and his measured responses to the actions of others accomplished their purpose. As Marion realized in Section III, Charlie is in control of the situation, and is on the point of reclaiming his daughter and redeeming his honor. But as the events of the climax show, Charlie's tactics are not enough. But by this time, his self-control is no longer just a tactic; it is clearly a habitual ethical strategy based on a strong belief in the "eternally valuable element," character. By the end of the story, he realizes that "there was nothing he could do" about the remote and recent past, nor about the future: he is neither a pessimist nor an optimist, but a realist. From the beginning, he has known that he wanted Honoria, and in Section III, "He was sure now that Lincoln Peters wanted him to have his child." Looking back on his experience he also realizes that Marion has yielded before, and may very well yield again. Finally, as he sits in the Ritz bar considering his victories and defeats, he becomes "absolutely sure Helen wouldn't have wanted him to be so alone." All of his experiences during the last few days in Paris suggest to him that it is only a matter of time, perhaps Lincoln's "six months," before the swing of the past will have lost its momentum.

A large measure of the success of "Absolution," "The Freshest Boy," and "Babylon Revisited" depends on Fitzgerald's ability to portray accurately and convincingly the inner life of the characters who inhabit the stories. He has drawn, as it were, a believable picture of souls in motion. To control this motion, he has created a deep structure which traces the characters' most profound thoughts and emotions; and in these stories, he has provided a map, the structural metaphor, so that the reader may follow the motion of these souls. Using this map, the careful reader will be able to discover and feel that "special emotion" and "special experience" that is at the heart of the stories and at the center of Fitzgerald's art.

NOTES

1. *As Ever, Scott Fitz—*, ed. Matthew J. Bruccoli (New York: J. B. Lippincott Co., 1972), p. 221.

2. *Ibid.*

3. *Ibid.*

4. The fourteen stories are: "Absolution," "Babylon Revisited," "Between Three and Four," "Crazy Sunday," "Flight and Pursuit," "The Freshest Boy," "Head and Shoulders," "John Jackson's Arcady," "Myra Meets His Family," "New Types," "A Nice Quiet Place," "Pat Hobby's College Days," "The Smilers," and "Too Cute for Words."

5. *The Price Was High*, ed. Matthew J. Bruccoli (New York: Harcourt, Brace, Jovanovich, 1979), p. xvi. Fitzgerald "scrapped" "Flight and Pursuit," "John Jackson's Arcady," "Myra Meets His Family," "New Types," and "The Smilers."

6. *Ibid.*, p. xii.

7. The discussion of the stories begins with "Absolution" only because it was written before the others. There is of course a temptation to see the three stories as the three ages of "Fitzgerald-Man": youth, adolescence, and maturity.

8. John A. Higgins, *F. Scott Fitzgerald: A Study of the Stories* (New York: St. John's Univ. Press, 1971), p. 67.

9. The most extreme development of the relationship between *The Great Gatsby* and "Absolution" occurs in Joan M. Allen, *Candles and Carnival Lights: The Catholic Sensibility of F. Scott Fitzgerald* (New York: New York Univ. Press, 1978). She imagines that "as Jay Gatsby he [Rudolph] will try to create his own amusement park, and like a squire who has prayed through the night of his childhood, he will assume the role of a knight in pursuit of the grail he imagines Daisy Fay to be" (p. 101).

10. Higgins, p. 67.

11. All quotations from "Absolution," "The Freshest Boy," and "Babylon Revisited," are taken from F. Scott Fitzgerald, *Babylon Revisited and Other Stories* (New York: Charles Scribner's Sons, 1971).

12. The "error" is discussed in J.I. Morse, "Fitzgerald's *'Sagitta Volante in Dei'*: An Emendation and a Possible Source," *Fitzgerald-Hemingway Annual* (1972), 321–322.

13. These translations, and all subsequent translations are mine.

14. F. Scott Fitzgerald, "Sleeping and Waking," *Esquire*, 2 (December, 1934), 34.

15. *Ibid.*

16. A very literal translation of *"negotio perambulante in tenebris"* ("business moving around in the darkness") might suggest the Ferris wheel.

17. The Latin verses of the Psalm were taken from *Biblia Sacra, Vulgatae Editionis* (Paris: Librarie Garnier Freres, N.D.), p. 577.

18. The quotation from *Summa Theologica*, II, ii, 1, 8, was taken from Josef Pieper, *Belief and Faith* (Chicago: Henry Regnery Co., 1963), p. 103.

19. Kenneth Eble, *F. Scott Fitzgerald* (Boston: Twayne Publishers, 1977), p. 26; Higgins, p. 107.

20. In an interview with Charles C. Baldwin, Fitzgerald said that while in boarding school, he "saw a musical comedy called 'the Quaker Girl' and from that day forth my desk bulged with Gilbert and Sullivan librettos and dozens of notebooks containing the germs of dozens of musical comedies." A shortened version of the interview is printed in *F. Scott Fitzgerald: In His Own Time: A Miscellany*, ed. Matthew J. Bruccoli and Jackson R. Bryer (The Kent State Univ. Press, 1971), pp. 267–270.

21. Higgins, p. 142.

22. Seymour Gross, "Fitzgerald's 'Babylon Revisited,'" *College English* (November, 1963), 128–135.

23. *Ibid.*, 130.

24. *Ibid.*, 131.

25. *Ibid.*, 135.

26. Gross, "Fitzgerald's 'Babylon Revisited,'" 135, points out the symbolic action of the pendulum image and its connection to the swing image.

27. Higgins, pp. 123–124.

28. Thomas F. Staley, "Time and Structure in Fitzgerald's 'Babylon Revisited,'" *Modern Fiction Studies*, 10 (1964–1965), 388.

29. Gross, "Fitzgerald's 'Babylon Revisited,'" 134, suggests "It is Charlie's own past that he is trying to force backward into time."

LEONARD A. PODIS

Fitzgerald's "The Diamond as Big as the Ritz" and Hawthorne's "Rappaccini's Daughter"

In his recent biography of F. Scott Fitzgerald, Matthew Bruccoli comments on the significance of the subtitle of a draft copy of *Tender Is the Night* and speculates as to its source: "The subtitle 'A Romance' indicates that Fitzgerald regarded his book as a departure from the realistic . . . modes of fiction. . . . It is not known whether Fitzgerald was familiar with Hawthorne's explanation of his designating *The House of [the] Seven Gables* a romance, but Fitzgerald's application of the term accords with Hawthorne's. . . ."[1] Similarly, a number of critics have attempted to link Hawthorne and Fitzgerald, particularly through themes, moods, characters, or techniques that appear in their work.[2] In this essay I will examine what strikes me as strong parallels between Hawthorne's "Rappaccini's Daughter" and Fitzgerald's "The Diamond as Big as the Ritz."

It is likely, but not provable, that Fitzgerald was familiar with "Rappaccini's Daughter."[3] Thus Elsa Nettels's statement in her recent article comparing Fitzgerald's "Babylon Revisited" and Howells's "A Circle in the Water" seems appropriate in describing the relationship between Fitzgerald and Hawthorne as well: "There is no evidence that Fitzgerald ever read 'A Circle in the Water,' but if he did not, it is all the more suggestive of affinities between the two writers that without knowing it Fitzgerald should write a story so similar in plot, situation and character. . . ."[4] In particular, comparing

From *Studies in Short Fiction* 21, no. 3 (Summer 1984): 243–50. Copyright © 1984 by Newberry College.

"Rappaccini's Daughter" and "The Diamond as Big as the Ritz" emphasizes the connection between Hawthorne and Fitzgerald as "romancers" who share an affinity for "departure from the realistic … modes of fiction" and a vision that tends to categorical extremes.

In both stories the plot centers on the entrance of a young man into an enchanted, yet poisonous, environment. The young protagonists, John T. Unger and Giovanni Guasconti, both students away from home, are attracted by the magical realm they have entered, and both find themselves drawn to entrapped young women (Kismine Washington/Beatrice Rappaccini). But as the courtship proceeds, their initial captivation turns to literal captivity as the reality of their own entrapment becomes clear. In addition to the beautiful, captive daughter and the perplexed, love-stricken suitor, both stories feature a dominant, ruthless father (Braddock Washington/Dr. Rappaccini). More important, both stories involve a powerful but morally ambiguous force (wealth/science) which ideally should liberate human beings but in fact imprisons them—a force which produces evil that is attractive, even seductive. Finally, Hawthorne and Fitzgerald rely extensively on fantasy to convey the truth of their vision.

Whatever the ultimate cause of the evil in the stories—perverted human nature or the excesses of a particular society—the immediate agents are clear: the science of Dr. Rappaccini and the wealth of the Washingtons. It is also obvious that both the science and the wealth are morally ambiguous. Each initially appears to be good, not evil; each has wondrous potential and has wrought dazzling creations. Although the beauty and splendor of Rappaccini's garden and the magnificence of the Washingtons' estate soon emerge in a sinister light, both are initially sources of great wonderment and fascination to the protagonists.

Giovanni's first extended glimpse of Rappaccini's "lovely and luxuriant vegetation" suggests the enchanted beauty of the garden:

> A little gurgling sound ascended to the young man's window, and made him feel as if the fountain were an immortal spirit that sang its song unceasingly. … All about the pool into which the water subsided grew various plants, that seemed to require a plentiful supply of moisture for the nourishment of gigantic leaves, and, in some instances, flowers gorgeously magnificent. There was one shrub in particular, set in a marble vase in the midst of the pool, that bore a profusion of purple blossoms, each of which had the lustre and richness of a gem; and the whole together made a show so resplendent that it seemed enough to illuminate the garden, even had there been no sunshine.[5]

Clearly, a romantic intensity suffuses this passage in which Giovanni is captivated by the garden's splendor.

Similarly, Fitzgerald's John Unger is initially enraptured by the radiance and splendor begotten by the Washingtons' enormous wealth on a barren mountainside:

> Full in the light of the stars, an exquisite chateau rose from the borders of the lake, climbed in marble radiance half the height of an adjoining mountain, then melted in grace, in perfect symmetry, in translucent feminine languor, into the massed darkness of a forest of pine. The many towers, the slender tracery of the sloping parapets, the chiselled wonder of a thousand yellow windows with their oblongs and hectagons and triangles of golden light, the shattered softness of the intersecting planes of starshine and blue shade, all trembled on John's spirit like a chord of music.[6]

The "honeyed luxury" is here no less appealing, and ultimately no less evil, than the magnificent richness of Rappaccini's garden.

As controllers of the morally ambiguous forces, both Dr. Rappaccini and Braddock Washington are, for their authors, embodiments of the danger in carrying a potential good to its evil inverse. Not only were the shrubs which grew under Rappaccini's sway marvelous in their beauty, but they helped him to effect "marvellous cures." Yet through Giovanni's "critical eyes" we are shown how the garden changes to a thing of evil. The flowers appear frightening,

> . . . as if an unearthly face had glared at him out of the thicket. Several also would have shocked a delicate instinct by an appearance of artificialness indicating that there had been such commixture, and, as it were, adultery, of various vegetable species, that the production was no longer of God's making, but the monstrous offspring of man's depraved fancy, glowing with only an evil mockery of beauty. (p. 128)

In "The Diamond as Big as the Ritz" the transformation of beauty into an evil mockery is accomplished through John Unger's gradually increasing awareness of the enormity of the Washingtons' crimes against humanity.

No less compelling and ambiguous than their fantastic creations are the arrogant Dr. Rappaccini and Braddock Washington themselves. If Rappaccini is a nineteenth-century mad scientist whose excesses warn us of the dangers of placing head above heart, Washington is his twentieth-century counterpart—a rampant capitalist who illustrates the ugliness of placing money and luxury above what Fitzgerald called "the old values": moral integrity, self-discipline, love for one's family, and regard for one's fellow human beings. At the root of each character's behavior is the uncontrollable urge to have and exercise power.

Braddock Washington's power is a consequence of his being the richest man in America. But his power is so great that he can proclaim autonomy from America and transcend the label "American." According to Percy Washington, "This is where the United States ends, father says" (p. 10). In order to achieve this powerful autonomy, the Washingtons have done unspeakable evil—plundering, kidnapping, murdering without remorse. Braddock Washington's father, in order to protect his wealth, established the tradition of keeping the estate a secret—thus it is on "the only five square miles of land in the country that's never been surveyed" (p. 10). The family's efforts to conceal the estate increasingly involve power more godlike than the simple bribery practiced by Washington's father when he "corrupted a whole department" of the U.S. government. Braddock Washington effectively changes the face of the land on a grand scale, diverting rivers and creating magnetic fields powerful enough to alter the instrument readings of surveyors.

Not only is the Washingtons' power increasingly godlike, but in their efforts at maintaining their secret empire, their power is increasingly exercised in its own service. Braddock Washington stresses, for example, that he would be willing to release the two dozen aviators he keeps imprisoned if there were some way of guaranteeing that they would not reveal his secret. But there is none, and in holding them prisoners he is forced to exercise a power he does not relish in order to retain the power which allows him to get away with such a thing in the first place.

In the words of one recent commentator, Dr. Rappaccini is "arrogant, ruthless, and cunning, but above all he is obsessed with power, the power to intimidate and control."[7] Of course, the chief source of Rappaccini's power is his science. We, as readers, must concur with Baglioni that Rappaccini possesses an "insane zeal for science" (p. 137) and that "he cares infinitely more for science than for mankind" (p. 116). Like Aylmer in "The Birthmark," a story which treats similar themes, Rappaccini is enamored of science primarily for the power it gives him. Aylmer, when boasting of his science to his wife, exclaims that "no King on his guarded throne could keep his life" if Aylmer chose to deprive him of it.[8] Similarly, Rappaccini, when the magnitude of his experiment with Beatrice and Giovanni finally becomes known, chastises Beatrice for renouncing the power with which his science has endowed her: "gifts against which no power nor strength could avail an enemy—... to be able to quell the mightiest with a breath—" (p. 147). As he delivers these words, "with a triumphant expression," Rappaccini's own "bent form grew erect with conscious power" (p. 146).

Like Braddock Washington, Rappaccini lives in large measure for the object of his obsession—a power to control the most powerful of men, if he so desires, and a godlike power to create and shape physical elements and natural forces. Braddock Washington's enormous wealth, power, and resources lead him to believe ultimately that he can bargain directly with God. In so doing, he echoes both Aylmer's and Rappaccini's statements about controlling the world's most powerful men, promising that he will slay "for the amusement of the Divine Benefactor any victims He should choose, even though it should be the greatest and most powerful man alive" (pp. 34–35). Rappaccini's intoxication with his own skills leads him to attempt the creation not only of magical shrubs, but of a new order of human life in the pairing of Giovanni and Beatrice. Spreading his hands over them as if he were God blessing Adam and Eve, he exclaims:

> "My science and the sympathy between thee and him have so wrought within his system that he now stands from common men, as thou dost, daughter of my pride and triumph, from ordinary women. Pass on then, through the world, most dear to one another and dreadful to all besides!" (pp. 146–47)

Indeed, Giovanni has earlier wondered, "Was this garden, then, the Eden of the present world?" (p. 112).

But the "upshot" of Rappaccini's experiment is that, like Braddock Washington, he has wrongheadedly exercised his power, not only in the name of evil, but in the service of itself, in a tribute to his own "perverted wisdom." When Washington's attempts to play God proved inadequate, he attempted to bribe God with wealth and tributes that he alone on earth could offer. Although the attempt at bribery failed, it signifies that Washington held fast to his perverted vision to the last. Similarly, despite the undesirable upshot of his life's work, Rappaccini clings to his science and trusts in himself to the end. Although the folly and evil of both characters is clear to the reader, and to certain characters in the stories, neither Washington nor Rappaccini ever breaks faith with his obsession.

The motifs of imprisonment and entrapment that figure prominently in "The Diamond as Big as the Ritz" and "Rappaccini's Daughter" arise from similar circumstances. Although the Washingtons are geographically more isolated in their uncharted portion of Montana, Dr. Rappaccini has effectively cut off his Paduan garden from the outside world. In both cases the isolation, with its attendant imprisoning effects, is enforced to insure the secrecy and security of the father's obsession. And in each case the intrusion of the protagonist, who also serves to establish the point of view, sets up the final entrapment.

As characters through whose eyes much of the action is seen, John Unger and Giovanni Guasconti do differ in important respects. While John is rather shallow and glib, Giovanni is sensitive and brooding. Yet, John is not presented as particularly unreliable; we have little reason to question his view of events. Giovanni's reliability, however, is frequently suspect. At one point, too much wine "caused his brain to swim with strange fantasies in reference to Dr. Rappaccini . . ." (p. 118). The narrative voice later states that Giovanni was able "to observe, or imagine" (p.119). Similarly, we learn that "his imagination ran riot continually," producing "wild vagaries" (p. 122).

Still, both young men are appropriate point-of-view characters. It is precisely Giovanni's "wonder-working fancy," his romantic disposition, which makes him receptive to Rappaccini's mysterious activities. Likewise John Unger's reverence for wealth and material success—instilled in him in his Midwestern hometown of Hades and reinforced by his attendance at St. Midas's School, "the most expensive and the most exclusive boys' preparatory school in the world" (p. 6)—makes him receptive to Washington's powers. It was chiefly the prospect of beholding the Washingtons' wealth that lured John west in the first place: "That [Percy Washington] was wealthy went without saying, so it promised rich confectionery for his curiosity when Percy invited him to spend the summer . . ." (p. 6).

But besides being receptive, both characters can also be appropriately critical by virtue of their being victimized. Both can be seen as the unwilling pawns of power figures. As was mentioned earlier, in both cases the young men are drawn to entrapped daughters only to discover subsequently their own entrapment. John falls in love with Kismine Washington, who, though privileged with every luxury imaginable, and even some "beyond human wish or dream," is effectively cut off from significant relationships with anyone outside her immediate family. Her father permits only occasional summer guests to visit the estate, and these, unfortunately, must then be permanently "removed" so that they won't divulge the secret. As Kismine tells John, "In August usually—or early September. . . . They were drugged while they were asleep—and their families were always told that they died of scarlet fever in Butte" (p. 27). Because she knows that her association with a friend would prove fatal to that person, she has never invited a guest, preferring isolation to being the cause of someone's death. Giovanni falls in love with Beatrice Rappaccini, who, though she rejects the evil power afforded her by her father, none the less is prevented from forming friendships and love relationships. Like Kismine she is cut off from normal human interaction. As Beatrice tells Giovanni, "'my father's fatal love of science . . . estranged me from all society of my kind. Until Heaven sent thee dearest Giovanni, oh, how lonely was thy poor Beatrice!'" (p. 143). To Beatrice, Rappaccini's "marvellous gifts" are a "miserable doom." And it is not merely Kismine's childishness which makes her exclaim near the end of "The Diamond as Big as the Ritz," "'We'll be poor, won't we? Like people in books. And I'll be an orphan and free. Free and poor! What fun!'" (p. 32).

Attracted to the lonely daughters, the suitors soon discover that they are in danger. John finds out that he must pay for his visit to the Washingtons with his life. Upon learning that he is to be murdered like all the other visitors to the estate, he accuses Kismine of both complicity and duplicity:

> "And so," cried John accusingly, "And so you were letting me make love to you and pretending to return it, and talking about marriage, all the time knowing perfectly well that I'd never get out of here alive—." (p. 27)

Kismine responds with wounded righteousness:

> "No," she protested passionately. "Not any more. I did at first. You were here. I couldn't help that, and I thought your last days might as well be pleasant for both of us. But then I fell in love with you. . . ." (p. 27)

Similarly, when Giovanni discovers "the awful doom" he must endure for having loved Beatrice, he accuses the object of his love of complicity in the scheme:

> "Accursed one!" cried he, with venomous scorn and anger. "And, finding thy solitude wearisome, thou hast severed me likewise from all the warmth of life and enticed me into thy region of unspeakable horror!" . . .
> "Yes, poisonous thing!" repeated Giovanni, beside himself with passion. "Thou has done it! Thou hast blasted me! Thou hast filled my veins with poison!" (p. 143)

In defense of her innocence and her love for Giovanni, Beatrice denies his accusations:

> "No, no, Giovanni; it was not I! Never! never! I dreamed only to love thee and be with thee a little time, and so to let thee pass away, leaving but thine image in mine heart. . . ." (pp. 144–45)

At one level we might explain the similarities in these stories by observing that both authors have coincidentally drawn on archetypal figures and patterns: the domineering father, the mad scientist, the isolated daughter, the love-blinded suitor, the fall of the over-reacher, the danger in tampering with nature, etc. Be that as it may, the similarities do seem to go beyond mere coincidence to suggest a visionary kinship between the two authors.

Neither work is really a cautionary tale in any practical sense. Clearly Hawthorne did not intend "Rappaccini's Daughter" as a warning to would-be scientists, nor did Fitzgerald write "The Diamond as Big as the Ritz" to discourage people from pursuing great wealth and luxury. But in a broader, more symbolic sense, both stories are cautionary in their treatment of human excesses. Both Hawthorne and Fitzgerald are concerned with the potential for evil that attends misplaced priorities and with the attractiveness of that evil.[9] For Hawthorne this takes the form of a brooding, metaphysical consideration of the upshot of Rappaccini's Faustian efforts. For Fitzgerald, it takes the form of a more tongue-in-cheek social criticism of the Washingtons' behavior. In each case the criticism is tempered by the authors' awareness of their characters' strengths. At their best, both Rappaccini and Washington are shown to be gods, who, appropriately, work wonders on a divine scale. Consequently, as we have seen, both stories contain a central ambiguity.

It is also significant that both authors rely heavily on fantasy.[10] In each story, the presence of fantastic abilities or the occurrence of fantastic events aids the authors in creating the central ambiguity; fantasy enables them to sketch both the best and the worst possibilities and to do so in the extreme. Fantasy contributes, in "Rappaccini's Daughter," to the depiction of a science that is not merely good or useful, but magnificent and transcendent in its powers; likewise it enables the presentation of a science that is not merely bad or dangerous, but malevolent and monstrous. By the same token, fantasy better enables Fitzgerald to sketch the power of great wealth as alternately ineffable and nightmarish.

"Rappaccini's Daughter" and "The Diamond as Big as the Ritz" appear to be linked, then, not only by their plots, situations, and characters, but by a common romantic vision. Both are informed by a similarly extreme, categorical way of seeing human endeavor and its potential for good or evil. In the case of these two stories it is thus quite reasonable to assert that Fitzgerald's fictive approach indeed "accords with Hawthorne's. . . ."

NOTES

1. *Some Sort of Epic Grandeur* (New York: Harcourt Brace Jovanovich, 1981), pp. 342–43, 343n.

2. See, for example, Kenneth Dauber, *Rediscovering Hawthorne* (Princeton: Princeton University Press, 1977), pp. 157 and 171, who suggests a relationship in

point of view between *The Blithedale Romance* and *The Great Gatsby*; Brian Way, *F. Scott Fitzgerald and the Art of Social Fiction* (New York: St. Martin's Press, 1980), p. 58, who views Hawthorne's Zenobia as an ancestor of Fitzgerald's flapper; Henry Dan Piper, *F. Scott Fitzgerald: A Critical Portrait* (New York: Holt, Rinehart and Winston, 1965), p. 296, who sees an affinity between Hawthorne's and Fitzgerald's conceptions of the importance of time; and Sergio Perosa, *The Art of F. Scott Fitzgerald* (Ann Arbor: University of Michigan Press. 1965; rpt. 1968), pp. 191–93, who asserts that "a 'vertical' examination of the origins of American tradition" shows a kinship between Hawthorne and Fitzgerald in their concern for the self and self-awareness. Perosa offers perhaps the most comprehensive comparisons of Hawthorne and Fitzgerald, suggesting links between, among others, *The Scarlet Letter* and *The Great Gatsby* (pp. 61–62), *The Scarlet Letter* and "The Fiend" (pp. 136–37), *The Marble Faun* and "A Short Trip Home" (p. 86), and "The Celestial Railroad" and sketches in *Afternoon of an Author* (pp. 141–42).

3. For useful discussions of Fitzgerald's reading and of the generally acknowledged literary influences upon his work, see Lawrence Buell's "The Significance of Fantasy in Fitzgerald's Short Fiction," in *The Short Stories of F. Scott Fitzgerald: New Approaches in Criticism, ed. Jackson R. Bryer* (Madison: University of Wisconsin Press, 1982), pp. 34–35 and Way, pp. 22–25.

4. "Howells's 'A Circle in the Water' and Fitzgerald's 'Babylon Revisited,'" *Studies in Short Fiction*, 19 (Summer 1982), 262. Consider also Way's assertion (p. 25) that "the discussion of Fitzgerald's place in the American literary tradition depends far more on the recognition of affinities than the mechanical charting of influences."

5. Nathaniel Hawthorne, "Rappaccini's Daughter," in *Mosses from an Old Manse*, Vol. II of *The Works of Nathaniel Hawthorne* (Boston: Houghton, Mifflin, 1882), p. 111. Subsequent references appear in the text.

6. F. Scott Fitzgerald, "The Diamond as Big as the Ritz," in *The Stories of F. Scott Fitzgerald* (New York: Scribner's, 1951), p. 11. Subsequent references appear in the text.

7. Richard Breeze, "Beatrice Rappaccini: A Victim of Male Love and Horror," *American Literature*, 48 (1976), 161.

8. "The Birthmark," in *Mosses from an Old Manse*, Vol. II of *Works*, p. 59.

9. See Perosa, p. 86: "If the obsession with evil of [Hawthorne] is echoed in the supposed singer of the Jazz Age, it is only because Fitzgerald has turned to his own bitter experience for inspiration. . . ."

10. Hawthorne's use of the fantastic is of course widely acknowledged. Buell's recent article, cited above, argues convincingly that fantasy plays a more important role in Fitzgerald's writing than has been generally recognized.

ROBERT ROULSTON

Fitzgerald's "May Day": The Uses of Irresponsibility

For a story so good, "May Day" is remarkably bad. Fitzgerald acknowledges its most flagrant fault in his Preface to *Tales of the Jazz Age*. After stating that the story is based upon three unrelated events, he concludes that he tried "unsuccessfully . . . to weave them into a pattern" (viii). Furthermore, as Richard D. Lehan notes, the action is "badly motivated" and "unconvincing and melodramatic" (84–85). Even the generally brilliant writing often strains too hard after cleverness and sometimes merits complaints about its coarseness and intrusive irony (Tuttleton 191; Sklar 78). Yet if Henry Dan Piper goes farther than most critics when he extols it as Fitzgerald's finest work before *The Great Gatsby* (69–71), the consensus is that "May Day" is one of his better efforts. Both Matthew J. Bruccoli (141) and Kenneth Eble (56) rank it among his very best stories. Sergio Perosa finds the technique "masterful" (32). Even those who rate it lower invariably place it above numerous other stories with more plausible events and more compact structures.

Many of the flaws of "May Day" result from its being a combination of incongruous elements. Part traditional fiction and part avant-garde, it combines plot devices characteristic of Fitzgerald's early *Saturday Evening Post* stories with themes of the less popular pieces that appeared in *The Smart Set*. It also juxtaposes naturalism and satire. It has some of the breadth of the

From *Modern Fiction Studies* 34, no. 2 (Summer 1988): 207–15. © 1988 by Purdue Research Foundation.

novel it was originally to have been and the concentration of the successful short story. It is alternately funny and sad, ludicrous and disturbing—a discordant piece that captures the silliness and pathos, the banality and vitality of the Jazz Age, whose opening it heralds and dramatizes. As in a Charles Ives symphony, where hymn tunes collide with passages from Beethoven, the effect is simultaneously crude and stimulating. Faults become inseparable from virtues, and the lack of synthesis is part of the message.

Fitzgerald should not have been surprised when *The Saturday Evening Post* rejected "May Day."[1] Few stories would seem less likely to have appealed to the magazine's morally conservative, probusiness editor, George Horace Lorimer. After all, it opens with a parody of the Bible and ends with a suicide. In between are riots, debauchery, a sordid liaison, and a monstrous marriage. One character gets his leg broken; another is shoved from a window to his death. Throughout nearly everyone is intoxicated, as Fitzgerald offers mordant comments on rich and poor, reactionaries and radicals.

Such fare was patently closer to the tastes of H. L. Mencken, the iconoclastic editor of *The Smart Set*, who published the story in July 1920 after it had been spurned by editors of all the large-circulation magazines (Bruccoli 141). Yet in certain respects "May Day" is closer to the six Fitzgerald stories the *Post* published in 1920 than to most of his other works that appeared in *The Smart Set*.[2] Not only is it more plotted than *The Smart Set* pieces usually are, but the narrative pivots about the central device of the *Post* stories, the mismatched couple—a congenial subject, no doubt, because of Fitzgerald's difficulties at the time with Zelda. Sometimes the obstacle—as in "Myra Meets His Family," "Head and Shoulders," and "The Offshore Pirate"—is a disparity in wealth or social status. In "The Camel's Back" the impediment is temperamental incompatibility. In "The Ice Palace" different regional backgrounds divide the pair. In the sixth *Post* story, "Bernice Bobs Her Hair," the heroine's small-town provinciality brings her into conflict with both male and female members of the country-club set in a large midwestern city.

In "May Day," therefore, Gordon Sterrett, trapped in a relationship with a proletarian Circe, Jewel Hudson, has the kind of problem that confronts the heroes of the early *Post* fiction. So, too, does Peter Himmel, who escorts Gordon's old flame, Edith Bradin, to a fraternity dance at Delmonico's Restaurant in New York, only to be rebuffed by her before he sets off on a binge with another Yale man, Phil Dean. The rejection and the subsequent bacchanalian capers are reminiscent of events in "The Camel's Back."

In many of the early *Post* stories, however, the plots are so farcical or improbable that Fitzgerald can resolve narrative dilemmas in them through a sequence of ever more absurd twists leading to preposterous and usually comic culminations. Thus, in "The Camel's Back," a supposedly mock-wedding ceremony between the heroine, disguised as a snake charmer, and the hero, concealed in the front half of a camel suit, turns out to have been valid. In "The Offshore Pirate" and "Myra Meets His Family," Fitzgerald contrives elaborate hoaxes that he needs only to expose to their victims in order to provide the happy endings Lorimer preferred.[3] "Bernice Bobs Her Hair" also concludes on an upbeat note, as does "The Ice Palace" after the southern heroine endures her ordeal in a northern winter.

In "May Day" all the story lines end unhappily. Gordon Sterrett, blackmailed by his vulgar mistress, wakes from a drunken stupor to find himself married to her. He then shoots himself. Peter Himmel and his drinking partner, Phil Dean, climax their debauch by soaring pointlessly in an elevator to the top of the Biltmore Hotel wearing In and Out signs stolen from the cloakroom of Delmonico's. In a third narrative line, two recently discharged veterans, Gus Rose and Carrol Key, crash a party at Delmonico's, where Key's brother is a waiter, and later join a mob in an attack on a socialist newspaper edited by Edith Bradin's brother, Henry. Key gets shoved to his death, and Gus breaks Henry Bradin's leg.[4]

The unhappy endings in "May Day," however, are as contrived as the happy ones in the early *Post* stories. Too many characters happen to be at the right place at the right times, and Sterrett's collapse and destruction occur too precipitously. His compromising letters to Jewel Hudson are an implausible device to put him in her power; furthermore, his marriage to her is as unbelievable as anything in "The Offshore Pirate." Where did they get a marriage license so quickly? Who would have officiated while the groom was so inebriated he could barely stand erect? Where did Sterrett's pistol come from? Would a young man just three years out of Yale and from a good family be in such desperate straits? It is also unlikely that Peter Himmel would be dating the very girl Sterrett has been pining for, that she in turn would be the sister of the editor whose office is attacked by Gus and Carrol, whose brother works at Delmonico's—and so forth, as the coincidences mount as high as the Biltmore where just about everyone shows up including Gus, who, for no discernible reason, is there exactly when Edith comes in and recognizes him as the man who has broken her brother's leg.

So many improbabilities would devastate an entire novel by Theodore Dreiser or Frank Norris. "May Day," on the other hand, not merely survives them; it flourishes in part because of them. While not exactly a fantasy, Fitzgerald's story is phantasmagoric with a nightmarish, drunken hallucinatory quality that can accommodate barely credible events. In this regard, as in others, it more resembles *Post* farces like "The Camel's Back" and "Heads and Shoulders" than it does naturalistic fiction, resonances of Dreiser and Norris notwithstanding.[5]

Too much has been made of such resonances. Lehan, in particular, believes that the influence of Norris is a major cause of the melodrama and implausibility of both "May Day" and *The Beautiful and Damned* (41–42). But an important difference exists between the story and Fitzgerald's novel. *The Beautiful and Damned*, like Norris's *McTeague* and *Vandover and the Brute*, writhes along from episode to episode, the main structural principle being the protagonist's downward trajectory. All three books abound in extraneous incidents and descriptions. In "May Day" Gordon Sterrett may plunge like Vandover, but Sterrett is no mere naturalistic hero, just as the story as a whole is no Norris-like boa constrictor bulging with indigestible prey. Although some of the themes of "May Day" savor of Norris and of Norris's advocate, H. L. Mencken, the overplotted narrative suggests Fitzgerald's recent *Post* stories.

Unlike Lorimer of the *Post*, Mencken preferred loosely structured fiction. In fact, five years later, in defending *The Great Gatsby* against Mencken's charge that the novel is hardly more than an anecdote, Fitzgerald contended that he had written the book as a protest against the formless works Mencken liked.[6]

Although Mencken's influence is undoubtedly present in "May Day," it should not be overestimated. Many Menckenesque features of the story— flippancy, scoffing at authority, admiration for superior people, contempt for incompetent lower orders, and disdain for plutocrats—abound in undergraduate stories Fitzgerald had written when, as he himself stated, Mencken had been "little more than a name" (*Correspondence* 55). To be sure, throughout his career Fitzgerald would acquire ideas and techniques second-hand from conversations, book reviews, and imitative works. And even before 1920 Mencken had been so famous that Fitzgerald must have had some inkling of what Mencken had been advocating.

But whether as a result of direct influence or of a fortuitous convergence of sensibilities, "May Day" does reveal certain clear affinities with Mencken. James W. Tuttleton may be correct in perceiving Mencken's impact upon the style. Certainly the "hyperbole, the high-flown rhetoric and the archaisms" Tuttleton cites savor of the master (19). Even more redolent of Mencken are the flippant asides, as when Fitzgerald describes Edith Bradin's dreamy state after prolonged dancing as "equivalent to a noble soul after several long highballs" (98). Fitzgerald here is indulging in the kind of Prohibition bashing that led Mencken to propose to "abolish all the sorrows of the world by the simple device of getting and keeping the whole human race gently stewed" ("Portrait of an Ideal World" 389).

Even more characteristic of Mencken is Fitzgerald's barb about Henry Bradin, the socialist editor, having come to New York "to pour the latest cures for incurable evils into the columns of a radical newspaper" (86). Fitzgerald's thrust at socialism resembles Mencken's assault on Thorstein Veblen's critique of capitalism as a "wraith of balderdash" ("Professor Veblen" 73). Furthermore, Fitzgerald's description of that pair of *Untermenschen*, Gus Rose and Carrol Key—the one "swart and bandy-legged," the other with a "long, chinless face ... dull, watery eyes ... without a suggestion of either ancestral worth or native resourcefulness" (74)—are like Mencken's jibes at "the weak and the botched" and disdain for the "simian gabble of the crossways" he encountered in Dayton, Tennessee, while covering the Scopes trial for *The Baltimore Sun* ("In Memoriam: W. J. B." 66).

Despite scattered Menckenesque touches, however, the dialogue, syntax, and even the tone of "May Day" are not substantially different from their equivalents in Fitzgerald's *Post* fiction of 1920. One finds the same briskness and brashness, fondness for brittle ironic banter, and bursts of colorful rhetoric. A stylistic difference, however, between "May Day" and, say, "The Ice Palace" or even the frivolous "The Offshore Pirate" is that whereas in these *Post* stories Fitzgerald permitted himself passages of unabashed lyricism, in "May Day" the cynicism is relentless. Thus he defaces with a sneer the most beautiful passage in the story, the marvelous evocation of morning light coming through the window of Child's Restaurant: "Dawn had come up in Columbus Circle, magical breathless dawn, silhouetting the great statue of the immortal Christopher, and mingling in a curious and uncanny manner with the fading yellow electric light inside" (99). Robert Sklar is right: Fitzgerald has robbed the passage of "romantic wonder" with his daub of irony (78).

Yet Fitzgerald's reluctance to evoke "romantic awe" in such a story is understandable. He would later envelop Jay Gatsby and Dick Diver in shimmering prose because he wanted to invest them with glamour. In "May Day," on the other hand, he deflates not just buffoons like Gus Rose and Peter Himmel but precisely the sort of characters he exalts elsewhere. Thus Edith Bradin, a potential Daisy Fay, is a narcissist whose language is "made up of the current expressions, bits of journalese and college slang strung together into an intrinsic whole, careless, faintly provocative, delicately sentimental" (85–86). She is also given to admiring her own face and figure and telling herself that she smells sweet and is "made for love" (86). Sterrett, a failed artist, stumbles about in a perpetual alcoholic fog, with blood-streaked eyes and trembling hands—more contemptible than pathetic as he wallows in self-pity. Lest any reader confer undue respect upon Edith's idealistic brother, Fitzgerald deflates him with the denigratory comments previously cited and underscores his disdain by adding that Edith, "less fatuously" than Henry Bradin, wants to cure Sterrett rather than the "incurable evils" of society (86).

More striking even than the wedding of Menckenesque sarcasm with *Saturday Evening Post* material is Fitzgerald's blend in "May Day" of traditional narrative methods with innovative ones. James R. Miller, Jr., too readily accepts Fitzgerald's claim that he had no model for the technique of the story. Miller is right, however, in noting how the technique anticipates what John Dos Passos would later do and in observing that Fitzgerald would not employ this approach again (53–56). In 1920, however, the use of parallel stories loosely connected, yet in some measure autonomous, was hardly unprecedented. Elizabethan dramatists frequently resorted to such plots, and like Fitzgerald they would intermix comedy with tragedy.

A search, however, for an earlier practitioner of this kind of storytelling need not extend back beyond the nineteenth century. There, right in the heart of Victorian England, loomed Charles Dickens, his novels bursting with plots, subplots, and parallel plots—all with melodrama cheek and jowl with low comedy. Dickens' contemporary, Thackeray, whose influence on *Gatsby* Fitzgerald acknowledged,[7] was also given to multiple plots. So was Leo Tolstoy, whose twin crisscrossed story lines in *Anna Karenina* foreshadow the contrasting fates of Sterrett and Dean. Similarly, the concluding part of Dreiser's *Sister Carrie* shifts back and forth between Carrie ascending toward stardom on the stage and Hurstwood, her lover, sinking lower until he commits suicide in a flophouse. In short, "May Day" looks back to Dickens, Thackeray, Tolstoy, and Dreiser as much as it looks forward to Dos Passos. In one important sense, in fact, it is closer to nineteenth-century fiction than to most serious twentieth-century writing. Fitzgerald binds together his narrative strands with unlikely encounters between characters in a manner reminiscent of Dickens but that would have been alien to Joyce, Hemingway, or Faulkner.

Yet "May Day" seems modern in a way that the *Post* stories and even *The Great Gatsby* and *Tender Is the Night* do not. Much of that avant-garde aura comes from the pacing of the story more than from the structure. In 1920—and indeed long afterwards—modernity meant angularity, jaggedness, disconnectedness. It meant the dissonance of Stravinsky, the distortions of Picasso, the fragmentation of Joyce and Eliot. In *This Side of Paradise* Fitzgerald made some gestures toward this type of sensibility by altering his narrative method from section to section much as Joyce had done in *A Portrait of the Artist as a Young Man* and would soon do on an even grander scale in *Ulysses*. But like most great modernists Joyce used rigorously applied methods to give new forms to his apparent chaos. Fitzgerald, however, in *This Side of Paradise* arbitrarily switches from prose to poetry and from dialogue to narrative, tossing in undergraduate pieces here and afterthoughts there. The result is a modernistic manner without the innovative substance of Joyce and

Eliot. Fitzgerald, in truth, was never a radical in aesthetics any more than in politics. When he rebelled, he was likely to produce what Edmund Wilson perceived in *This Side of Paradise* as "a gesture of indefinite revolt" (79) rather than a sustained assault on authority and convention.

A similar gesture pervades "May Day." The cynical asides, the mocking preface, and the fragmented narrative do not obliterate the conservatism that was always a part of Fitzgerald's character. Just as Gordon Sterrett and Edith Bradin look back nostalgically on their own prewar days, so Fitzgerald reaches back to traditional forms of fiction. The story is less an experiment in form than a speeded-up version of a nineteenth-century novel with multiple plots, chance encounters, theatrical climaxes, and tidy denouements. The effect, however, of forcing into a few pages what Dickens would have put in hundreds is that of a motion picture film run at high speed. All is jerky, ludicrous, and surreal. "May Day," then, becomes a frenzied film clip of the birth of the Jazz Age. Its disparate elements, juxtaposed so daringly, do not coalesce and should not, because underlying both the action and the language are two irreconcilable emotions—disgust and élan. Perhaps only a story that should not be taken altogether seriously could adequately capture simultaneously this incongruous pair of attitudes that, in their very incompatibility, seem to capture the *Zeitgeist* of the early 1920s. Fitzgerald, of course, was already becoming the self-proclaimed bard of that *Zeitgeist* and was well upon his way toward viewing himself as both its exemplar and its victim.

Much of the disgust, hence, is self-disgust of the sort that made Fitzgerald exclaim in 1921 to Maxwell Perkins: "I'm sick of the flabby semi-intellectual softness in which I flounder with my generation" (*Letters* 148). Even in that outburst, however, he viewed his own weakness as symptomatic of a larger malaise. In "May Day" he directs his disgust at nearly every target in sight. The largest target is the central event of the story, the May Day riots of 1919, which he would recall a decade later with rancor.

> When the police rode down the demobilized country boys gaping at the orators in Madison Square, it was the sort of measure bound to alienate the more intelligent young men from the prevailing order. We didn't remember anything about the Bill of Rights until Mencken began plugging it, but we did know that such tyranny belonged to the jittery little countries of South Europe: ("Echoes of the Jazz Age" 13)

But, if the brunt of Fitzgerald's disgust here would seem to fall upon the authorities and their minions, in "May Day" hardly any group escapes it. Wealthy Phil Dean is a profligate and a cad. Plebeians Gus Rose and Carrol Key are subhuman. One of the two major female characters is a low-class temptress; the other is a shallow upper-class flirt. The socialists are naive fools; the Ivy League graduates are self-centered debauchees. Waiters, like Carrol Key's brother, are sycophants. History, embodied in the statue of Columbus, is derided; the future is a pointless ride up an elevator to a nonexistent floor as Dean and Himmel scream "higher" to the operator after reaching the top. And through all the folly and selfishness flows a ceaseless stream of alcohol. Sterrett's suicidal alcoholism, of course, is a lurid enlargement of Fitzgerald's own growing drinking problems, just as Dean's and Himmel's drunken prank with the In and Out signs from Delmonico's is a fictionalized version of one of Fitzgerald's binges with a fellow Princetonian, Porter Gillespie (Turnbull 95–96).

Indeed, Fitzgerald imposed some of his own less attractive qualities on various characters in "May Day." Sterrett shares not just his creator's weakness for liquor but also his self-pity. And just as Sterrett berates himself for failing to become an artist, so Fitzgerald complained constantly about the hackwork that kept him from writing serious fiction. Dean's vanity about his shirts and ties resembles Fitzgerald's sartorial snobbery. Even the lowly Carrol Key is akin to Fitzgerald in more than one way. Key's last name suggests that, like Francis Scott Key Fitzgerald, he is descended from the author of "The Star Spangled Banner." The first name also links him to the Maryland aristocracy to which Fitzgerald's father belonged. If the Fitzgeralds of Minnesota had not declined through "generations of degeneration" like Key's forebears (74), they were certainly less splendid than their Tidewater ancestors had been.

Yet despite the disgust directed at patricians and paupers, past and future, humanity and himself, Fitzgerald does not make "May Day" an orgy of nihilism. Perhaps he does not because Mencken had taught him to laugh at the world more than to rage at it. The Baltimore burgher was too much the sybarite to demolish the pleasant things in life to get at the bad ones. Similarly, for all his pessimism, the young man who wrote "May Day" had too much zest for living to surrender to the despair warranted by some of the events he depicts. "May Day," in fact, captures the *carpe diem* exuberance Ernest Hemingway was to depict on a grander scale in *The Sun Also Rises*. Thus the anguished Sterrett, like the melancholy Robert Cohn, seems a colossal party-pooper. His troubles are real enough but are largely self-induced, and nothing in his demeanor or conduct is very prepossessing. He bawls and complains and reels about with rolling, bloodshot eyes. No doubt his college friend, Phil Dean, is being a bounder by refusing him the three hundred dollars Sterrett needs to meet Jewel Hudson's demand. Yet Sterrett is "bankrupt morally as well as financially" (66), Jewel would certainly repeat her blackmail, and Sterrett appears incorrigible. Thus, under the circumstances, Dean's behavior is not unreasonable. He has come to New York for a holiday, and Sterrett is spoiling his fun. Like the botched Carrol Key, Sterrett is symptomatic of those "incurable evils" only foolish idealists like Henry Bradin worry about.

And so, in the bizarre carnival atmosphere of "May Day," Sterrett's chamber of horrors is counterbalanced by the crazy-house revelry of the irresponsible Phil Dean and his equally irresponsible cohort, Peter Himmel. Sterrett's alcoholic nightmare is antithetical to the "warm glow" Himmel experiences after his third highball when he feels as though he were "floating on his back in pleasant water" (95). Looking at the crowd on the street, Dean and Sterrett have opposite responses to the "display of humanity at its frothiest and gaudiest." To Dean the struggle is "significant, young, cheerful"; to Gordon it is "dismal, meaningless, endless" (71). As Sterrett's already low fortunes decline even farther, Himmel and Dean soar to a manic state where everything becomes hilarious, and the wildest caprice seems feasible. Why not wear cloakroom signs? Why not threaten bodily harm to a waiter at Child's? Why not toss hash at the customers? Why not have liquor with breakfast? And why stop riding up an elevator even after reaching the top floor of the Biltmore?

Fitzgerald, to be sure, was no more a Dean or Himmel than he was a Sterrett, albeit pieces of himself went into all three characters, just as other pieces went into Key or even into the radical Henry Bradin. (After all, Amory Blaine, the hero of the largely autobiographical *This Side of Paradise*, claims to be a socialist.) Yet in at least one respect Dean and Himmel are closer than the other characters to the heart of "May Day." Their irresponsibility is perfectly attuned to the giddy pace, the capricious grafting together of genres, and the flippant comments throughout. Sterrett or Bradin could never have written "May Day." A talented Himmel or Dean just might have.

The sensibility that pervades Fitzgerald's later works, however, is remote from Himmel's. By the mid-1920s, when much of his own *joie de vivre* had waned, Fitzgerald would adopt the more somber point of view of Nick Carraway for *The Great Gatsby*. At the end of the decade Charles Wales, disgusted by his own and his friends' dissipation, would provide the focal point of "Babylon Revisited," Fitzgerald's sad epilogue to the Jazz Age. In the prologue to that era, "May Day," however, youth cavorts, and wet blankets are thrown aside with more sneers than tears.

Notes

1. Fitzgerald, however, may well have been disappointed by the *Post*'s rejection of the story. After all, while writing "May Day" in November of 1919, he queried his agent, Harold Ober, about "The Ice Palace": "Do you think this is *Post* stuff?" (*As Ever* 5). The answer was a resounding yes. But for all its beauty and power, "The Ice Palace," unlike "May Day," is a straightforward narrative with a single,

sharply defined conflict, one grand climax, and a reassuring denouement. When its southern heroine flees from her northern boyfriend and his family, she returns to her own milieu and to her own kind; thus all seems well. Throughout humor is injected lightly and is seldom malicious. The writing is lyrical; the symbolism rarely bizarre. The story, in other words, is a smooth performance that makes its points clearly and inoffensively.

2. Evidently, Fitzgerald wrote no stories specifically for *The Smart Set*. Although he diagrammed plots of *Post* stories in order to learn what the magazine wanted (Turnbull 287), his pieces that appeared in *The Smart Set* had generally been rejected by better paying periodicals. Many, too, were undergraduate efforts originally published by Princeton's *Nassau Literary Magazine*. These included slapdash parodies like "Mister Icky," banter-filled sketches like "Babes in the Woods," and cynical vignettes like "Tarquin of Cheapside."

3. Lorimer might have tolerated *one* of these endings. In 1931 he published Fitzgerald's "A New Leaf," where the protagonist, who resembles Gordon Sterrett, leaps to his death from an ocean liner. But even in that story the heroine marries a more proper suitor to provide a more positive final touch.

4. Fitzgerald's plot in "Myra Meets His Family" is not unlike the one he jeers at in *The Vegetable* when he has his ignorant hero recommend a story in the latest issue of the *Post*: "Read the one about the fellow who gets shipwrecked on the Buzzard Islands and meets the Chinese girl, only she isn't a Chinese girl at all" (10). The island setting, however, is reminiscent of "The Offshore Pirate." Fitzgerald may have derived the title of his play from Mencken's jibe at the *Post*: "Here is a country in which it is an axiom that a business man shall be . . . a reader of *The Saturday Evening Post*, a golfer—in brief, a vegetable" ("On Being an American" 96).

5. The comic nature of many of the episodes serves another purpose. It gives Fitzgerald a license denied to realism in its more somber modes. After all, from Terrence and Plautus to William S. Gilbert and Oscar Wilde, timely coincidences and startling revelations have added to the laughter. In "May Day" the drunken antics of Gus Rose and Carrol Key and the escapades of Dean and Himmel at Child's—where they toss hash at the other customers and later at the Biltmore and Commodore Hotel dining rooms where they demand champagne with breakfast—are as farcical as anything in "The Camel's Back," one of Fitzgerald's more inane *Post* stories.

6. In his review of *Gatsby* in *The Baltimore Evening Sun*, (2 May 1925: 9), Mencken praised Fitzgerald's writing but contended that the story is thin and contrived and that the novel should not be "put on the same shelf" as the plotless *This Side of Paradise*. Fitzgerald's remarks are in a letter to Mencken, 4 May 1925, in response to correspondence from Mencken containing similar criticism of *Gatsby* (*Letters* 480).

7. The acknowledgement is in a letter to John Jamieson, 7 April 1934 (*Letters* 509).

Works Cited

Bruccoli, Matthew J. *Some Epic Sort of Grandeur: The Life of F. Scott Fitzgerald*. New York: Harcourt, 1981.

Eble, Kenneth. *F. Scott Fitzgerald*. New York: Twayne, 1963.

Fitzgerald, F. Scott. *The Correspondence of F. Scott Fitzgerald*. Ed. Matthew J. Bruccoli and Margaret M. Duggan. New York: Random, 1980.

———. "Echoes of the Jazz Age." *The Crack-Up*. Ed. Edmund Wilson. New York: New Directions, 1956. 13–22.

———. *The Letters of F. Scott Fitzgerald*. Ed. Andrew Turnbull. New York: Scribner's, 1963.

———. "May Day." *Tales of the Jazz Age*. New York: Scribner's, 1922. 61–125.

———. *The Vegetable: Or from President to Postman*. 1923. New York: Scribner's, 1976.

Fitzgerald, F. Scott, and Harold Ober. *As Ever, Scott Fitz: Letters Between F. Scott Fitzgerald and His Literary Agent, Harold Ober*. Ed. Matthew J. Bruccoli and Jennifer M. Atkinson. Philadelphia: Lippincott, 1972.

Lehan, Richard D. *F. Scott Fitzgerald and the Craft of Fiction*. Carbondale: Southern Illinois UP, 1966.

Mencken, H. L. "In Memoriam: W. J. B." *Prejudices: Fifth Series*. New York: Knopf, 1922. 64–74.

———. "On Being an American." *Prejudices: A Selection*. Ed. James T. Farrell. New York: Vintage, 1959. 89–125.

———. "Portrait of an Ideal World." *A Mencken Chrestomathy*. Ed. H. L. Mencken. New York: Knopf, 1949. 388–391.

———. "Professor Veblen." *Prejudices: First Series*. New York: Knopf, 1919. 59–82.

Miller, James E., Jr. *The Fictional Techniques of Scott Fitzgerald*. The Hague: Martinus Nijhoff, 1957.

Perosa, Sergio. *The Art of F. Scott Fitzgerald*. Ann Arbor: U of Michigan P, 1968.

Piper, Henry Dan. *F. Scott Fitzgerald: A Critical Portrait*. New York: Holt, 1965.

Sklar, Robert. *F. Scott Fitzgerald: The Last Laocoon*. New York: Oxford UP, 1967.

Turnbull, Andrew. *Scott Fitzgerald*. New York: Scribner's, 1962.

Tuttleton, James W. "Seeing Slightly Red: Fitzgerald's 'May Day.'" *The Short Stories of F. Scott Fitzgerald: New Approaches in Criticism*. Ed. Jackson R. Bryer. Madison: U of Wisconsin P, 1982: 181–197.

Wilson, Edmund. "Fitzgerald Before *The Great Gatsby*." *F. Scott Fitzgerald: The Man and His Work*. Ed. Alfred Kazin. 1951. New York: Collier, 1962. 78–84.

BRUCE L. GRENBERG

"Outside the Cabinet-Maker's": Fitzgerald's "Ode to a Nightingale"

Like many of Fitzgerald's lesser known, seldom anthologized short stories, "Outside the Cabinet-Maker's" has a somewhat baffling critical history. Written in 1927 during the Fitzgeralds' turbulent stay at Ellerslie, outside Wilmington, Delaware, and offered to seven different magazines before finally being published by *Century* magazine in December 1928, the story was not included in *Taps at Reveille* and remained virtually unnoticed until Arthur Mizener reprinted it in *Afternoon of an Author*, with a brief but suggestive interpretive headnote.[1] With its rebirth in Mizener's widely read collection, and its additional reprinting in volume 5 of *The Bodley Head Scott Fitzgerald* and in Mizener's edition of *The Fitzgerald Reader*, the story finally began to receive some critical notice in the 1960s and early 1970s.

Indeed, in the nine-year period from 1962 to 1971, Andrew Turnbull, Henry Dan Piper, Sergio Perosa, and John A. Higgins all made favorable comment upon the story in one way and another; nevertheless, for the past twenty years, "Outside the Cabinet-Maker's" has been almost totally neglected in critical studies of Fitzgerald's work. Matthew J. Bruccoli's *Some Sort of Epic Grandeur*, notable for its inclusiveness of detail, does not mention the story, and in Alice Hall Petry's *Fitzgerald's Craft of Short Fiction* (which deals with Fitzgerald's *collected* short stories) the story is summarily treated in a single sentence with four other "pre-1935 stories that had not been included in

From *New Essays on F. Scott Fitzgerald's Neglected Stories*, edited by Jackson R. Bryer, pp. 118–29. © 1996 by the Curators of the University of Missouri.

the four collections." More recently, the story has received "honorable mention" in two books on Fitzgerald. Bryant Mangum finds in the story's "brevity and compactness" a precedent for Fitzgerald's "new style" in the 1930s. John Kuehl holds a similar view of the story's stylistic significance, seeing in the "detached exclusive" style of "Outside the Cabinet-Maker's" the precursor of the ironies found in "Babylon Revisited."[2]

In his headnote to the story in *Afternoon of an Author*, Mizener sets the basic assumptions and terms of reference for all the early commentators. Citing the autobiographical origins of the story, he rightly notes Fitzgerald's "intense and incommunicable" love for his daughter and sees the story as a "characteristic example of the way Fitzgerald transmuted actuality to make it true." And certainly Mizener is also right when he observes that the story is a "brilliant manifestation of the acceptance of the loss Fitzgerald would never cease to feel." But he also sets a dangerous and misleading precedent for the criticism to follow by concluding that "the story has the basic simplicity of plan and the care to be explicit, to make no unnecessary mysteries for the reader, that Fitzgerald always aimed at."[3] This assumption of the story's "simplicity" is erroneous in itself, and, more seriously, it has debilitated all subsequent criticism.

Andrew Turnbull was the first to reflect Mizener's reductive assumptions and reading. Ignoring the boundary between life and art, Turnbull mistakenly views "Outside the Cabinet-Maker's" as an exclusively autobiographical sketch recounting a pleasurable moment between Fitzgerald and Scottie during their time at Ellerslie: "'You're my good fairy,' said Fitzgerald [sic] smiling and touching Scottie's [sic] cheek." Sergio Perosa is more perceptive, viewing "Outside the Cabinet-Maker's" as a "beautiful little sketch, which shows what delicacy of feeling and bareness of style Fitzgerald could attain." Perosa relates the story not to Fitzgerald and Scottie, but to Dick Diver and his children in *Tender Is the Night*. And Henry Dan Piper views "Outside the Cabinet-Maker's" as one of Fitzgerald's "most perfect stories," finding in "its charm, its precision of language and image, its cool detached humor and affection" a foreshadowing of "such notable essays as his 'Crack-up' [sic] pieces, 'The Lost Decade,' 'Author's Home,' and 'Afternoon of an Author.'"[4]

John A. Higgins presents some cogent reasons for viewing this neglected short story as a superb example of Fitzgerald's fiction. Higgins argues that "Outside the Cabinet-Maker's" is "unlike any other piece of its author's short fiction before 1935," and sees in the story's "objectivity, implication, and ratio of dialog" an "almost ... complete reversal of [Fitzgerald's] typical pattern." Higgins attributes this radical change to the influence of Hemingway upon Fitzgerald at that time and cites signal similarities between Fitzgerald's story and Hemingway's "episode pieces" such as "A Clean, Well-Lighted Place."

Higgins claims, finally, that Fitzgerald, indeed, "had manifested the whole of what would become his 'new' technique in 'Outside the Cabinet-Maker's.'"[5] But Higgins adheres tightly to his main concern with Fitzgerald's techniques and confines his comments on the story to matters of style, scarcely discussing the story's themes or dramatic power.

Even though these "early" commentaries by Mizener, Turnbull, Perosa, Piper, and Higgins are progressively laudatory—suggesting intricate connections between the story and Fitzgerald's life, artistic theory, and practice in the late 1920s—the seeds of these ideas have been slow to germinate. Even Kuehl and Mangum, who genuinely admire the story, use it merely as a springboard to their critical comments about Fitzgerald's style, apparently assuming that such a simple little story is essentially self-explanatory, however finely constructed. The reason for this untoward suspension of critical activity, I think, is that we have placed the critical cart before the horse; we have had premature agreement about the story's autobiographical, canonical, and stylistic implications before we have adequately debated its intrinsic concerns and values. What is ultimately lacking in the existent criticism, and what I hope to provide in this essay, is a detailed analysis of the story's central thematic concerns. For far from being simple, "Outside the Cabinet-Maker's" is intricately wrought; and though I cannot hope to find the bottom of Fitzgerald's art in the story, I do hope that my comments will stimulate further inquiry into a work that has been allowed to lie fallow for far too long.

For the most elemental reasons, "Outside the Cabinet-Maker's" should be of more than casual or peripheral interest to Fitzgerald scholars, for it was written almost exactly midway between the publication of *The Great Gatsby* and Fitzgerald's settling upon the plan for the new novel, which would become *Tender Is the Night*, that was giving him "the terrible incessant stop[p]ies" in 1927.[6] Accordingly, then, within the compass of this very short story Fitzgerald explores many of the themes that were at the center of *The Great Gatsby*, with its focus upon the dreamworlds of imagination and expectation (Gatsby's, Nick's, and Myrtle's) and their collisions, frequently violent, with the real worlds of experience and fact. The story also reveals Fitzgerald's preoccupation with the themes and values that become the center of *Tender Is the Night*, where the reality of mindless will and money clashes with idealism and a "willingness of the heart" to suspend belief in one's own experience. The story, in fact, succinctly expresses Fitzgerald's creative concerns in this most critical period in his career; for, ultimately, "Outside the Cabinet-Maker's" is about imagination itself—about its power and its limitations. It is Fitzgerald's latter-day "Ode to a Nightingale," in which he captures the essence of the "waking dream" of imagination and the forlorn nature of what Keats called "the sole self"—when that music is fled.

I agree with Piper and Higgins that "Outside the Cabinet-Maker's" is a most carefully crafted short story, and its brevity allows us a very sharply focused view of Fitzgerald's commitment at this point in his career to a fiction of form, exclusion, suggestion, and splendid intimation. Although Perosa is right when he says that "there is practically no action" in the story, he is right in a misleading way, for the story powerfully demonstrates Fitzgerald's sense of just how much can take place when there is "nothing happening."[7] Indeed, the story flourishes, and can flourish, only when the reader is willing to witness and accept Fitzgerald's incalculable "trick of the heart" that leads us through the minimal, indeterminate surface plot to the thematic center of the story. We, like the imaginary Prince of the story's fairy tale, are charged with the task of rescuing the beautiful Princess—imagination—from the curtained surface reality of the narrative.

We needn't dispute an autobiographical provenance to recognize that Fitzgerald intended a much broader and deeper significance in "Outside the Cabinet-Maker's." He purposefully expands the story's values by leaving the main characters unnamed—referring to them throughout the story as "the man," "the lady," and "the child," thus universalizing their roles and the values of their relationship. Fitzgerald expands the story yet further by placing the story's superficial "reality" in opposition to the subjective expectations and imaginings of the central characters. The most evident expression of this theme, of course, is the encompassing opposition between the actual events of the narrative and the imaginary world the man creates for the child while waiting for the lady to return to the car. But throughout the story there is a persistent, emphatic leitmotiv of oppositions, or interpenetrations, between reality and imagination that serves as a repeating pattern of the story's central concerns.

Thus, we note the anomalous contrast between the story's initial setting "at the corner of Sixteenth and some dingy-looking street" (137) and the conversation in French between the man and the lady as they decide upon a "maison de poupée" for their child. Similarly, the neighborhood is described both as "red brick" (138; or solid, fixed, immovable) and as "vague, quiet" (138; or indeterminate, suggestive). Furthermore, this neighborhood's ambiguous character gives rise to the man's fairy tale, which is in itself insubstantial yet founded upon the objective details of the neighborhood scene. "Darkies," clerks, and passersby become King's soldiers, a little boy becomes the Ogre, and, to cite a classic example of Fitzgerald's method of mingling fancy with fact, the man in the story affirms that the Prince in the fairy tale found one of the blue stones "in President Coolidge's collar-box" (139).

The dollhouse as central motivation in the story is, in itself, an object both of reality (with a set price of twenty-five dollars) and of imaginative promise (for the lady who never had one as a child, and for her child, who doesn't know she is getting one made for her). Further, and more conclusively, the whole imaginary world the man creates for the child means something far different to him than to the child, who actually *sees* the soldiers that her father can only imagine. In all these instances (and in many others throughout the story), Fitzgerald establishes a complex interdependency between a reality that appears fixed and a subjectivity of imagination and expectation that nevertheless attempts to give new shapes and purposes to that reality. And the dynamic modulations and displacements of the "objective" and the "subjective" in the story express Fitzgerald's definition of both the power and the limitations of imagination.

The protagonist and focal point of the story is the man, who, like the poet in "Ode to a Nightingale," clearly recognizes the ambiguity of living at once in the related but distinct worlds of reality and imagination. Almost always in Fitzgerald's fiction the dreams that are so compelling for the dreamers prove to be Keatsian dreams—transient, incomplete, and thus, ultimately, unsatisfying; in "Outside the Cabinet-Maker's" the man's acute awareness of his situation produces in the story both an intensity and a fragility of tone as he attempts to accommodate both worlds in his experience.

The man's journey into the realm of imagination begins inauspiciously enough. Waiting outside the cabinet-maker's on the "vague, quiet" street, "the man and the little girl looked around unexpectantly." After the child and man exchange perfunctory and conventional declarations of love, the man begins to make up a fairy tale to pass the time for himself and the child: "'Listen,' the man continued. 'Do you see that house over the way?'" (138). The story he makes up is, as a fairy tale, utterly derivative and conventional, or, if you will, archetypal. It includes an imprisoned Princess, an Ogre, a Prince who must complete a quest to free the Princess and restore order to the kingdom of the captive King and Queen, and so on. At the outset the man is only half-committed to his own creation, and his imagination falters: "'She [the Princess] can't get out until the Prince finds the three—' He hesitated." And when he is prompted by the child to complete the conditions of the quest ("The three—the three stones that will release the King and Queen"), he is overtaken by ennui—"He yawned" (138).

At this point in the story a deep sea change takes place. The fabricating fancy of the man is outrun and taken over by the imagination of the child, and from this point to the end of the story, the man finds himself in an unequal contest with the child, who can experience directly what the man can only invent. The man embellishes his tale with the assertion that the room will turn blue every time the Prince finds one of the three stones and thinks to titillate the child with the remark, "*Gosh!* . . . Just as you turned away I could see the room turn blue. That means he's found the second stone" (139). On the surface, the child's response seems innocent enough: "'Gosh!' said the little girl. 'Look! It turned blue again, that means he's found the third stone'" (139). But Fitzgerald is concerned with more than a child's echo of a parent's speech. Although the child's response reflects her father's fancy, as well as words (beginning with the exclamatory "Gosh!"), we are forced by Fitzgerald to recognize a critical distinction amid likeness. The child's echo, in fact, sounds more deeply and resonantly than her father's proclamation, for while he has merely represented the room as turning blue, she has *seen* it turn blue.

At this crucial juncture in the story, Fitzgerald underscores what is at stake for the man in an emphatic one-sentence paragraph: "Aroused by the competition the man looked around cautiously and his voice grew tense" (139). This sentence is at the center of the story and is, I think, the axis around which the story turns. Challenged by the child's envisioning imagination, the man is frightened by what he finds, or rather doesn't find, in himself—the capacity for believing in and directly experiencing a world of pure imagination. From this point in the story until the wife returns from the cabinet-maker's and reintroduces reality into the narrative, the man, like Nick in *The Great Gatsby* and Dick in *Tender Is the Night*, strains to recapture childhood's simple yet dauntless belief in a fairyland world that conforms to the expectations and anticipations of one's imagination.

The man's position is ambivalent, tenuous, and weighted with irony, yet Fitzgerald is able to compress the complex condition of his character in the simple question the man puts to his daughter: "'Do you see what I see?' he demanded" (139). Of course she doesn't, but at this point in the story he does try to see what *she* sees. He creates an Ogre out of a little boy walking along the street, but now instead of being writer, producer, and director of the drama being played out, the man joins the little girl as part of the audience: "They both watched" (139). And "the little boy" most improbably construed as an Ogre finally becomes that Ogre—for the child, the man, and even for the third-person narrator. If only for a moment, the imagined becomes the reality of the scene: "The Ogre [not 'the little boy'] went away, taking very big steps" (139).

This struggle of imagination to exert itself upon reality and, in effect, transcend it informs the falling action of the story. The resolution of the fairy tale hinges upon the outcome of the conflict between the bad fairies and the good fairies, who struggle for control over the shuttered window of the Princess's prison room. In the story's thematic terms, the struggle is between the vague stolidity of the neighborhood scene and the values invested in that reality by fancy and imagination. Finally, the conflict is played out within the man's ambivalent consciousness of being an adult inextricably bound to a world of inflexible reality and, at the same time, being irresistibly drawn to the imagined world of the child.

All the implications of the man's predicament conflate into his summary statement of the conflict between the bad fairies, who "want to close the shutter so nobody can see in," and the good fairies, who "want to open it" (140). In the story's terms, bad fairies are prohibitive—the conservative guardians of a reality viewed as impenetrable surface; and good fairies are liberating—inviting one to look beneath and beyond the surface of things to a richness of meaning that is as compelling as it is fleeting. Thus, the child's observation that "The good fairies are winning now" marks the ascendancy of creative imagination as it gives form to resistant reality, both in the fairy tale and in the story itself. And the man's response ("'Yes.' He looked at the little girl. 'You're my good fairy'" [140]) emphasizes Fitzgerald's abiding romantic conviction that the liberating, creative imagination is never and nowhere stronger than in the innocence of childhood.

As in Keats's "Ode to a Nightingale," however, that deceiving elf, imagination, "cannot cheat so well as he is famed to do," and the man is stricken by the realization that even while the little girl sits upon the throne of Queen Mab, "clustered around by all her starry Fays," *he* is doomed to "the weariness, the fever, and the fret" of his adult world: "The man was old enough to know that he would look back to that time—the tranquil street and the pleasant weather and *the mystery playing before the child's eyes, mystery which he had created, but whose luster and texture he could never see or touch any more himself.* Again he touched his daughter's cheek instead and in payment fitted another small boy and limping man into the story" (140; emphasis mine).

The man thus realizes he is exiled forever from the true mystery (that is, the miracle) of the child's imagination, and this realization produces in him a spontaneous declaration of love: "'Oh, I love you,' he said" (141). The words "I love you" are the same as those uttered at the beginning of the story, but they are now invested with a rich meaning, for the declaration of love springs not from the imprisoning authority of the parent ("Listen, ... I love you") but from the man's recognition that the child is, as Wordsworth would have it, "abundant recompense" for his own lost childhood. Or perhaps it is more accurate to say that for Fitzgerald the child is *almost* recompense for the man's lost youth: "For a moment he closed his eyes and tried to see with her but he couldn't see—those ragged blinds were drawn against him forever. There were only the occasional darkies and the small boys [not soldiers and not Ogres anymore] and the weather that *reminded* him of more glamorous mornings in the past" (141; emphasis mine).

This shock of self-recognition abruptly cuts off the flight of fancy that has taken him momentarily to the fairyland of the child's imagination, and it is precisely at this moment that "the lady came out of the cabinet-maker's shop" (141). Earlier, the man had described the lady on the street as "a Witch, a friend of the Ogre's"(140), and that definition has a resonant effect upon our view of *the* lady in the story. For her return to the car from inside the cabinet-maker's signals the man's irrecoverable return to the world of reality, his conversation with his wife turning immediately to matters practical and mundane, focusing upon the price of the dollhouse. The man's fall from grace is emphasized yet further by the fact that he must leave behind him the child, who remains in fairyland. With great concision, but bearing the cumulative force of the entire narrative with it, the final line of the body of the story is the haunting plea of the child: "Look, Daddy, there go a lot more soldiers!" (141).

The closing section of the story emphasizes a dualistic world in which reality and imagination, adulthood and childhood, are essentially discrete. And the last "paragraph-epilogue" serves not only as a narrative conclusion to the story but also as a summary gloss upon the values of the man, the lady, and the child: "They rode on abstractedly. The lady thought about the doll's house, for she had been poor and had never had one as a child, the man thought how he had almost a million dollars and the little girl thought about the odd doings on the dingy street that they had left behind" (141). This conclusion, however, provides an "overture" rather than a "closure" to the story's ultimate values, for it invites us to rethink and revalue the story from an altered perspective. The lady, who for the most part has been given form by her absence throughout the story, is now given a presence and at least a hint of definition. The man, who has been seen essentially as father of the child, now is seen as his "sole self." And the child, who has been depicted as responding to, though dominating, her father, is seen, for the first time, to be reflective. In these hints toward new directions, the final paragraph invites us to inquire more deeply into the "odd doings on the dingy street."

The salient revelations in this last paragraph are that the man has money and that the woman has had a "deprived" childhood. It is commonplace to comment upon Fitzgerald's preoccupation with money, but I am not sure we have valued properly yet the metaphorical, even symbolic, value of money in his works. Although his short stories and his novels are to a large degree founded upon money—upon people who have it and people who don't, people who dream about it and people who dream with it—money never remains just money in Fitzgerald's works; it becomes, rather, a symbolic means of revealing personality. Thus, the mention of the man's money in the last paragraph of "Outside the Cabinet-Maker's" is intrinsic rather than peripheral to our understanding of the man's character throughout the story. The revelation that the woman "had been poor" gives color and substance to our late-blooming thoughts about who she is and who she has been. And the revelations together give at least some definition to the relationship between husband and wife that is not made clear elsewhere in the story.

In a direct inversion of Fitzgerald's more typical plot depicting "the struggle of the poor young man to win the hand of the rich girl,"[8] in "Outside the Cabinet-Maker's" the poor young girl has won the hand of the rich boy, and perhaps because of this inversion it is easier to recognize Fitzgerald's symbolic use of money, not only in this story, but in his other fiction as well. Here, money is seen clearly, if implicitly, as a means of realizing one's dreams and giving substance to one's imagination. The lady who dreamed of, but never had, a dollhouse as a child can, thanks to her husband's wealth, buy one for her daughter and, we clearly sense, for herself. Indeed, in looking back upon the story we realize that all the lady's comments on the dollhouse are almost wholly restricted to its cost. Getting out of the car at the beginning of the story, she affirms, "I'm going to tell him it can't cost more than twenty dollars" (137); returning to the car at the end of the story, she says that it will cost "vingt-cinq" dollars and apologizes for taking so long (141).

If, in Fitzgerald's fiction, money is projected as the means of realizing personal dreams and is frequently depicted as an expression of the larger cultural American dream, he makes it clear in both story and novel that those individual dreams, like the national dream they embody, are inherently flawed. For Fitzgerald there is no reality, by definition, that can conform to the exquisite balance and harmony of winter dreams—or dreams outside the cabinet-maker's. The dollhouse in the mind of the lady and in the mind of the cabinet-maker will not and cannot be captured for twenty-five dollars or twenty-five thousand dollars.

As in all his great fiction, in "Outside the Cabinet-Maker's" Fitzgerald depicts money as a false lure that promises, but fails, to realize the soaring expectations of one's dreams. The man, who has been transported to the boundary of fairyland by his fairy child, returns with a crash at the end of the story to the anticlimactic reality of having "almost a million dollars," a phrase that at once conveys both completion and dissatisfaction; "almost a million dollars" is both a great deal of money and, we recognize with the man, not nearly enough. In Fitzgerald's fiction in general the adult's quest for material wealth is, indeed, a self-confounding attempt to supplant the lost ability of the child to experience dreams as actuality. Ultimately, in the ironic context of this story's final paragraph, "almost a million dollars" appears as the surviving fragment of an adult fairy tale with no fixed purpose and no happy destination in sight. At the story's end, the man, the lady, and the child "rode on abstractedly" (141).

The child, too, stands at the focal point of Fitzgerald's finalizing ironic vision, for the closing paragraphs suggest that the child is herself on the perilous brink of adulthood. Her resolution of the man's fairy tale is rooted in the death of the King, the Queen, and the Prince, and is expressed in her proclamation that "the Princess is Queen" and in her cheerful announcement that "she'll marry somebody and make him Prince" (141). The stakes involved in this transparently Freudian resolution are suggested by Fitzgerald quite clearly. The man, who "had liked his King and Queen and felt that they had been too summarily disposed of" (141), chastises his daughter: "'You had to have a heroine,' he said *rather impatiently*" (141; emphasis mine). But his unease, I suggest, arises not simply from his sense of lost authority, but from his deeper awareness of the condition underlying that lost authority—his child's loss of innocence and passage into adulthood. She too will become—at the very moment is becoming—an adult all too much like her parents.

The final sentence of the story tells us that the child "thought about the odd doings on the dingy street that they had left behind" (141). In that suggestive, compressed statement we see the first diminution of the child's unquestioning capacity for wonder and the first chilling hint of the adult's pained awareness of the intricate inseparability of "odd doings" and "dingy street[s]"—of imagination and the reality it feeds upon but cannot be nourished by.

Notes

1. Henry Dan Piper, *F. Scott Fitzgerald: A Critical Portrait*, 173.

2. Alice Hall Petry, *Fitzgerald's Craft of Fiction: The Collected Stories, 1920–1935*, 190; Bryant Mangum, *A Fortune Yet: Money in the Art of F. Scott Fitzgerald's Short Stories*, 153; John Kuehl, *F. Scott Fitzgerald: A Study of the Short Fiction*, 113–14.

3. F. Scott Fitzgerald, *Afternoon of an Author: A Selection of Uncollected Stories and Essays*, 137. All subsequent page references to "Outside the Cabinet-Maker's" are to this edition and will appear parenthetically in the text.

4. Andrew Turnbull, *Scott Fitzgerald*, 174; Sergio Perosa, *The Art of F. Scott Fitzgerald*, 95; Piper, *Fitzgerald: Critical Portrait*, 173.

5. John A. Higgins, *F. Scott Fitzgerald: A Study of the Stories*, 147.

6. Matthew J. Bruccoli, *Some Sort of Epic Grandeur: The Life of F. Scott Fitzgerald*, 263.

7. Perosa, *Art of F. Scott Fitzgerald*, 95.

8. Scott Donaldson, "Money and Marriage in Fitzgerald's Stories," 75.

J. GERALD KENNEDY

Figuring the Damage:
Fitzgerald's "Babylon Revisited" and Hemingway's "The Snows of Kilimanjaro"

During the pastoral interlude in *The Sun Also Rises* between the "fiesta-ing" in Paris and Pamplona, a sodden Bill Gorton harangues his fishing companion, Jake Barnes, about the destructive consequences of living abroad: "You're an expatriate. You've lost touch with the soil. Fake European standards have ruined you. You drink yourself to death. You become obsessed by sex. You spend all your time talking, not working. You are an expatriate, see? You hang around cafés" (119). The hypocrisy of his tirade hints at its satirical purpose. As a parody of Gertrude Stein's famous remark, "You are all a lost generation" (one of the novel's two epigraphs), Bill's indictment elicits from Jake a sarcastic retort—"It sounds like a swell life"— that insinuates Hemingway's mockery of Stein and his need to repudiate her authority.[1] Ironically, however, many of Bill's charges seem applicable to Jake, who in Book I spends far more time talking in Left Bank cafés than working in his office, who has developed "a rotten habit of picturing the bedroom scenes of [his] friends" (13), and who makes a fair effort, especially in Pamplona, to drink himself into oblivion. Presumably, Hemingway's growing ambivalence toward expatriate life, as reflected in his correspondence, gives the passage its doubly ironic rancor.[2]

Bill's blathering charge—which also smacks of 1920s Puritanism— nevertheless scants those aspects of literary exile in France that enabled

From *French Connections: Hemingway and Fitzgerald Abroad*, edited by J. Gerald Kennedy and Jackson R. Bryer, pp. 317–43. Copyright © 1998 by J. Gerald Kennedy and Jackson R. Bryer.

so many American writers to develop new voices and to launch important careers. In *A Moveable Feast*, Hemingway idealized Paris as "the town best organized for a writer to write in that there is" (182), and so the city must have appeared to scores of writers eager to escape oppressive influences back home. Repeated studies generally have celebrated expatriate life in Paris as liberating, productive, and transformative (Benstock, Carpenter, Ford, Kennedy, Pizer, and Wickes). But such perspectives privilege textual achievement, celebrate the public literary persona, and discount the personal calamities that occasionally attended the life caricatured by Bill Gorton. Although disasters can occur anywhere, and although geography seems at first glance irrelevant to the conduct of life, Paris nevertheless affected many American exiles (as Malcolm Cowley observed) like "a great machine for stimulating the nerves and sharpening the senses" (135). The escape from U. S. Prohibition; the greater range, availability, and acceptance of pleasures licit and illicit; and the practical advantage of a soaring exchange rate all combined with the wild exuberance of the 1920s (called in France *les années folles*) to encourage expatriate recklessness and risk-taking. Both Hemingway and his literary cohort, F. Scott Fitzgerald, later had occasion to assess the damage incurred during their years in France, and in memorable narratives written in the 1930s, each composed patently autobiographical meditations on loss and failure, on the costly profligacies associated with life abroad. Although Fitzgerald's "Babylon Revisited" and Hemingway's "Snows of Kilimanjaro" emerged from vastly different personal circumstances, both tend to deromanticize the antics of the Lost Generation by portraying scenes of self-confrontation and remorse. In each case, the protagonist's crisis leads to a reconsideration of the expatriate's "swell life" and raises unsettling questions about the ultimate influence of Paris, inscribed in both stories as a landscape of desire.

1.

The biographical context of "Babylon Revisited" possesses obvious relevance to the narrative itself. In March 1929, seven months before the great Wall Street Crash of 1929, the Fitzgeralds embarked on their last, catastrophic visit to France, and in April 1930, six months after Black Tuesday, Zelda Fitzgerald suffered an acute mental breakdown in Paris. After a period of observation and sedation at a facility in Malmaison, she decamped in angry defiance of her physician but shortly thereafter experienced the suicidal depression that led to her subsequent confinement at a Swiss psychiatric clinic (Bruccoli, *Epic Grandeur* 285). While Fitzgerald waited anxiously for news of his wife's treatment at Les Rives de Prangins in Nyon, he composed "Babylon" in December at a nearby hotel. The story appeared in the *Saturday Evening Post* two months later and belongs to a set of magazine stories (including "The Swimmers," "The Hotel Child," and "One Trip Abroad") issuing from that last trip to Europe and culminating in the publication of *Tender Is the Night* (1934). Like many a post-Romantic writer, Fitzgerald transformed private sorrows into public fables of loss, inventing tales about enervated American expatriates like himself, beset by failing marriages and complicated parental responsibilities. Discouraged by his wife's collapse, their long-strained marital relationship, and his inability to complete the new novel, Fitzgerald produced a handful of short stories that variously mirror the brokenness of his own life. As he dramatized his own sense of disintegration, he often placed his magazine characters in international dilemmas, torn between the seductiveness and moral laxity of postwar European cosmopolitanism and the quaint pieties of an earlier American way of life. Fitzgerald understood fiction as social mimesis and typically portrayed the breakdown of his jaded exiles as reflective of the broader historical and cultural shifts that marked the era of high modernism—the loss of certainty, the fading of traditional morality, and the rise of cultural relativism and skepticism.

Arguably, "Babylon" stands closest to *Tender* in its evocation of a profoundly tragic view of life, a point suggested by Fitzgerald's recycling of two key passages from the story in the longer work. As scholars and editors have often observed, the early description of Charlie Wales's melancholy taxi ride "through the tranquil rain" ("Babylon" 617), as well as his late, despairing realization that "he wasn't young any more, with a lot of nice thoughts and dreams to have by himself" (633), reappear in *Tender* to confirm the patent connection between Charlie's fall and that of Dick Diver, Fitzgerald's dashing yet ultimately defeated psychoanalyst-hero.[3] In both narratives, the writer implies an analogy between personal, domestic crisis and the stock market disaster of 1929.[4] Like Dick, Charlie yearns for the moral certainty of nineteenth-century America and wants "to jump back a whole generation" to "trust in character again as the eternally valuable element" ("Babylon Revisited" 619). Yet (again like Dick) he discovers the antithesis of that morally upright world in the alluring spectacle of Paris.

For Fitzgerald, as for his fictional American businessman, the city represented a scene of previous triumph. Writing to his wife in 1930, the author recalled his arrival five years earlier, shortly after the appearance of *The Great Gatsby*: "Then we came to Paris and suddenly I realized that it hadn't all been in vain. I was a success—the biggest man in my profession, everybody admired me and I was proud I'd done such a good thing" (*Life in Letters* 187). In 1925 he lived with his family at 14, rue Tilsitt, literally within the lengthened shadow of the Arc de Triomphe, a location that perhaps suited his momentary sense of literary conquest. Gertrude Stein hailed him and young

Ernest Hemingway envied him, soliciting his editorial advice about unpublished work. With a handsome income from stories published by the *Saturday Evening Post*, Fitzgerald lived like a rajah on the Right Bank. Similarly, Charlie Wales recalls with pleasure the economic power (born of advantageous exchange rates) enjoyed by expatriate Americans in Paris during the 1920s: "We were a sort of royalty, almost infallible, with a sort of magic around us" ("Babylon" 619). Americans unmistakably controlled the Ritz bar and seemed to own the city itself, as many a famous café underwent renovation to become a "*bar américain.*" Money made things happen: Charlie recalls "thousand-franc notes given to an orchestra for playing a single number, hundred-franc notes tossed to a doorman for calling a cab" (620). Fitzgerald himself had known that sense of power in which Paris figured as the symbolic reward for Yankee cleverness, an artificial paradise that, according to a new mythology of American exceptionalism, yielded its pleasures to the moneyed expatriate.[5]

Yet by 1930 Fitzgerald also regarded Paris as a place of debauchery and ruin. After the notorious summer of 1925, which in his addled memory consisted of "1000 parties and no work" (*Ledger* 179), his new friend Hemingway advised him: "Paris is poisonous for you" (*Selected Letters* 182). Fitzgerald nevertheless returned for extended, riotous visits in 1928 and again in 1929; he was living in the rue Pergolèse near the Porte Maillot, literally and figuratively on the far side of Triumph's Arch, when his wife collapsed from mental and physical exhaustion. During the months that followed, he left his nine-year-old daughter Scottie with a French governess while he languished in Switzerland reading Freud, writing stories, and waiting for reports from the psychiatric clinic. In that season of regret, Gay Paree may have seemed the very source and image of his misfortune. Suggestively Charlie Wales recalls the dissipation that marked his Paris years, especially the "terrible February night" that began with a scene at the Hotel Florida and ended when he locked his wife outside in a snowstorm. He realizes that he "lost everything [he] wanted" during the crazy years when too much easy money created a sense of fantasy, and men "locked their wives out in the snow, because the snow of twenty-nine wasn't real snow. If you didn't want it to be snow, you just paid some money" ("Babylon" 633). For Charlie, Paris is preeminently a scene of personal debacle, a locus of "utter irresponsibility" (629), and the central irony of his situation is that he must return to this "Babylon" to retrieve his nine-year-old daughter, Honoria, and whatever honor she may represent.

As Carlos Baker observed some years ago, Fitzgerald structures the action of the story around two opposed motifs—the "luxury and wickedness" of Babylon and the "quiet and decent home life" Charlie yearns to establish with his daughter (182). The genius of the story lies, however, in Fitzgerald's ability to insert these themes into a specific and suggestive cartography. From the outset, Paris itself embodies and reflects the contradictions that propel the hero back and forth between the Right Bank and the Left, between the Ritz bar and the Peters's apartment on the rue Palatine, as Fitzgerald charts a crucial topographical distinction. Charlie's negotiation of the city's geography—his movement within a symbolic landscape—suggests rather precisely the unfolding of an inner conflict that seems, in the final analysis, far more compelling than the custody battle with his sister-in-law, Marion Peters. At issue are three questions that suggest the uncertainty of his private situation. The most obvious of these concerns the extent of Charlie's recovery: Has he become a new man freed from his susceptibility to drink, or is he the old Charlie, still vulnerable to temptation, still parentally irresponsible? This is, of course, Marion's insistent suspicion, but the unflattering light in which she appears diminishes the apparent validity of her concern. Charlie moreover reassures her (and himself) that he has recovered, signaling this newfound self-control by the single, daily drink that demonstrates his sobriety. He thinks of the drink somewhat equivocally as the "spoonful of medicine" ("Babylon" 630) that preserves his emotional equilibrium, and throughout the story he adheres to this conscious regimen. Yet even as Fitzgerald insists on the self-discipline of his hero, he puts that recovery in question, and never more pointedly than when, during a tense scene at the Peters's, the narrator notes that "for the first time in a year Charlie wanted a drink" (626).

Fitzgerald elsewhere manipulates the geography of the story to suggest the insistence of Charlie's latent yearning for alcohol. Significantly, the narrative begins and ends at the Ritz bar (a place frequented by Dick Diver in *Tender* and habitually, in real life, by Fitzgerald himself), with Charlie taking his mandatory drink; the bar constitutes his refuge in Paris, the point of reference from which he gets his bearings. In the Ritz bar, significantly, he makes the Freudian slip that ultimately thwarts his effort to recover Honoria: A few lines into the story he asks the barman to give Lincoln Peters's address to Duncan Schaeffer, his old drinking pal, who at the wrong moment arrives drunkenly and unexpectedly on the rue Palatine with Lorraine Quarrles to derail the custody negotiations. Although Charlie pointedly declines to give Duncan and Lorraine the address when he encounters them in the second section of the story, still his "conscious volition"—the wish to avoid trouble—cannot finally protect him from the consequences of his initial parapraxis (Twitchell 156–60). A profoundly conflicted character, Charlie betrays the perverse, unresolved tension between conscious will and unconscious desire in his attraction to the Ritz. If his daily, self-consciously consumed drink "proves" his sobriety, the hastily scribbled address he leaves for Schaeffer betrays his irrepressible urge to reconnect himself with those lost years of bibulous gaiety.

A second, more complex question thus grows out of the first and concerns Charlie's relationship to the recent past: Does he at bottom regard "those crazy years" ("Babylon" 629) as an epoch of disastrous irresponsibility or as a period of freedom when "a sort of magic" and an ample bank account afforded him a charmed life? Charlie's insistent expressions of remorse seem to resolve the question, but his geographical movements betray conflicting attitudes. His wanderings around Montmartre at the end of the first section neatly reveal this divided sensibility, conveying the simultaneous attraction and repulsion that mark his relation to the past. After dining with the Peters family and Honoria on the Left Bank, Charlie decides "not to go home" but rather to revisit scenes of prior folly: "He was curious to see Paris by night with clearer and more judicious eyes than those of other days." His soirée includes a stop at the Casino de Paris (16, rue de Clichy) to watch Josephine Baker "go through her chocolate arabesques" (619) and a walking tour past Bricktop's, Zelli's, the Café of Heaven, and the Café of Hell. As the two Dantesque names suggest, his journey seems an exercise in self-reproach, evoking disgust: "So much for the effort and ingenuity of Montmartre. All the catering to vice and waste was on an utterly childish scale, and he suddenly realized the meaning of the word 'dissipate'—to dissipate into thin air; to make nothing out of something" (620). The nocturnal spectacle finally assumes a frightening, surreal quality, as Charlie discovers a Montmartre previously concealed by his own delusions of power and indestructibility. His perambulations invite us to consider the impulse that has lured him to the *quartier* of the place Blanche and that draws him back repeatedly to the Right Bank in this story of turning and returning.

The significance of this pattern lies in the contrast between the Right Bank, with its multiple associations of past hilarity, and the so-called provincial quality of the Left Bank, which in "Babylon Revisited" has nothing to do, curiously, with the expatriate hub of Montparnasse. Instead, Fitzgerald restricts his Left Bank to the rue Palatine—and by extension to the dour, ecclesiastical quarter that surrounds the Eglise St. Sulpice. Situated in the same neighborhood where the Fitzgeralds lived in 1928 and again in 1929, the address of the apartment refers explicitly to the Palatine Hills of Rome, linking the Peters to St. Peter and the Roman Catholic Church, an institution the lapsed Catholic Fitzgerald habitually associated with repression and guilt. All apartments on the short rue Palatine face the south facade of St. Sulpice—a circumstance that perhaps helps to explain the "fear of life" attributed to Marion Peters.

But as Carlos Baker has noted (271), an equally important association links the rue Palatine address with an earlier, pre-exilic home life. When Charlie enters the Peters's apartment, Fitzgerald notes: "The room was warm

and comfortably American" ("Babylon" 618). Marion Peters has once pos-
sessed "a fresh American loveliness," and in her presence Charlie immediately comments on the scarcity of their compatriots in Paris: "It seems very
funny to see so few Americans around" (619). At the Peters's, Charlie has an
instinctive sense of connection with his own national origins, with the familiar values of hearth and home, family and faith. But his antipathy for Marion
perhaps also betrays a converse expatriate scorn for conventional American
values, leaving him uncomfortable in this "provincial" space. Significantly,
after each of his three visits to the Peters's apartment, he departs immediately
for the Right Bank: On the first occasion, as discussed earlier, he wanders
Montmartre; on the second, he strolls back to his Right Bank hotel, feeling
"exultant" as he crosses the Seine; and on the third, he goes "directly to the
Ritz bar" (632). Thus, despite the moral outrage and shame evoked by Right
Bank scenes that recall a scandalous past, Charlie seems compelled to return
to those settings in which his life once seemed enchanted.

Fitzgerald shows the grip of this repetition mechanism in the story's
second section, when Charlie takes Honoria out for lunch and entertain-
ment. Throughout this scene, the action hovers between conscious banter and
unconscious desire, the father–daughter dialogue implying a flirtation that
dimly prefigures the incest theme in *Tender Is the Night*. Charlie has chosen
their dining place because it was "the only restaurant he could think of not
reminiscent of champagne dinners and long luncheons that began at two
and ended in a blurred and vague twilight" (620–21). But even as he tries to
escape the memory of his wild years, his choice of the elegant Grand Vatel
(275, rue du Faubourg St. Honoré) brings him back ineluctably to the Right
Bank, where—significantly—he encounters "sudden ghosts out of the past"
(622) in the persons of Duncan Schaeffer and Lorraine Quarrles. Although
Charlie refuses, in a gesture of will, to disclose the name of his hotel, he
does announce his next destination, the Empire music hall (41 avenue de
Wagram), a showplace also located on the Right Bank and comparable to the
Casino de Paris, which he had revisited earlier.[6] History repeats itself even as
Charlie tries to escape its influence. When Duncan and Lorraine show up at
the Empire, embodying the persistence and presence of the past, he agrees to
have a drink with them. In a symbolic sense he thus renews his connections
with the "crazy years" through a seemingly innocent excursion to two Right
Bank locations.

Fitzgerald sharpens the contrast between those opposing spheres of
meaning and experience, the Right Bank and the Left, in the fourth section
of the story with the arrival of the *pneumatique* from Lorraine that evokes
the remembrance of prior frivolity. The letter arrives at Charlie's hotel, having
been "redirected from the Ritz bar where Charlie had left his address for the

purpose of finding a certain man" (629). Fitzgerald pointedly refers to the mistake at the Ritz, yet his coyness here seems intriguing: By suppressing the name of Duncan Schaeffer, the narrator seems to participate in the hero's own psychic denial. The past that Charlie had unconsciously hoped to find has now found him, and Lorraine's note recalls a zany episode in which Charlie has pedaled a stolen tricycle "all over the Etoile"—that is, around the Arc de Triomphe—in the hours just before dawn. His recollection of the incident brings, however, no accompanying sense of triumph: "In retrospect it was a nightmare" (629).

Rejecting the invitation to meet Lorraine "in the sweat-shop at the Ritz"—at the geosymbolic nexus of the orgiastic past—Charlie thus proceeds to the Peters's apartment to conclude his custody talks with Marion. But in a brilliant scene that figures the intrusion of the "crazy years" into the present moment and the penetration of Right Bank revelry into the Catholic, provincial milieu of the place St. Sulpice, Fitzgerald stages the unexpected arrival of Duncan and Lorraine in the rue Palatine: "They were gay, they were hilarious, they were roaring with laughter. For a moment Charlie was astounded; unable to understand how they ferreted out the Peters' address" (631). In yet another allusion to his Freudian slip, he later tells Marion that Duncan and Lorraine "must have wormed [her] name out of somebody" (632). They know the address, of course, because Charlie has left it, perhaps subconsciously hoping to be rescued from cozy domesticity by his former companions in mirth. When Duncan makes the drunken suggestion that "all this shishi, cagy business 'bout your address got to stop" (631), he alludes to the crucial problem of place—to the question of where and how Charlie will situate himself within the city's symbolic landscape. Caught between the luxury and excess of the Right Bank and the provincial severity of the place St. Sulpice, simultaneously attracted to and repelled by both, Charlie finds himself now displaced within the paradise of exile.

This predicament seems linked to the third question Fitzgerald poses: Does Charlie repent his wayward past and accept responsibility for the losses he has suffered? The story's title here assumes particular significance, for the name "Babylon" recalls the seventy-year Babylonian captivity of the Israelites and the city's infamous association with international debauchery and decline: "Babylon was a golden cup in the Lord's hand, making all the earth drunken; the nations drank of her wine, and so the nations went mad" (Jeremiah 51:7). The great city which had once been an emblem of power and glory became through its own corruption "an object of horror among the nations" (Jeremiah 51:41). In the prophet Jeremiah's account, God causes Jerusalem to fall to King Nebuchadnezzar and subjects the Israelites to exile as punishment for their faithlessness and disobedience; God thus redeems the captives, paradoxically, by subjecting them to the greater wickedness of Babylon. By evoking the biblical city of sin that occasioned spiritual testing and penitence, Fitzgerald implicitly raises the question of whether Charlie himself performs penance and receives symbolic forgiveness or whether he remains an unrepentant exile.

Unmistakably the visit to Montmartre resembles a penitential journey, as when Charlie pauses before the Café of Hell and meditates on the word "dissipate," realizing that he has made "nothing out of something." He has "squandered" his money to forget "the things most worth remembering, the things that now he would always remember—his child taken from his control, his wife escaped to a grave in Vermont" (620). Later, at dinner at the Peters's, he assumes "the chastened attitude of the reformed sinner" but he does so, Fitzgerald notes, merely to "win his point" (625) with Marion. And he recoils defensively when she recalls the morning Helen arrived "soaked to the skin and shivering" (625) after Charlie had locked her out. Marion poses the central moral problem succinctly when she remarks: "How much you were responsible for Helen's death, I don't know. It's something you'll have to square with your own conscience" (627). Precisely so; Charlie's return to Paris produces an incessant struggle with conscience, projected symbolically upon the geography of the city. When he recalls "that terrible February night" that began on the Right Bank with a scene at the Hotel Florida (12, Boulevard Malesherbes) and ended with his locking out Helen, he implicitly denies responsibility: "How could he know she would arrive an hour later alone, that there would be a snowstorm in which she wandered about in slippers, too confused to find a taxi?" (628). Yet Lorraine's *pneumatique*, with its reference to the tricycle incident, awakens both memory and guilt: "How many weeks or months of dissipation to arrive at that condition of utter irresponsibility?" (629).

Charlie's struggle with penitence culminates in the final scene at the Ritz bar, when he confesses to the bartender that he has "lost everything [he] wanted in the boom" by "selling short" (633)—by sacrificing for the sake of momentary gratification what he should have treasured and husbanded. Yet Fitzgerald's famous formulation—"the snow of twenty-nine wasn't real snow" (633)—captures the radical ambiguity of the confession: Does Charlie blame himself for his actions, or does he attribute them to the unreal Zeitgeist of the 1920s? His subsequent self-pitying remark ("they couldn't make him pay forever" [633]) implies that he sees himself as more oppressed than culpable. He returns to Paris but fails to recover his daughter because he cannot elude Duncan and Lorraine, those personifications of recklessness; although he recognizes his general "irresponsibility," he never accepts blame for Helen's "escaping pneumonia by a miracle, and all the attendant horror"

(628). Failing to acknowledge responsibility for Helen's decline—or the need for contrition obliquely represented by the rue Palatine and the implied presence of the Eglise St. Sulpice—Charlie thus remains unrepentant and unabsolved. His visit to Paris forces him to confront the results of his carelessness, but unlike the Israelites he remains too deeply enamored of the pleasures of Babylon to recover his Honor(ia) or to escape the condition of spiritual exile. In a moment of brief moral insight, Charlie realizes: "I spoiled this city for myself" (618). He must therefore return to Prague to endure the captivity imposed by his own recalcitrance.

Whatever autobiographical freight the story finally carries, we must not, however, impute to Fitzgerald the moral obtuseness that afflicts Charlie Wales. Indeed, the author's subtle, recurrent reminders of his hero's fatal parapraxis comprise a lacerating self-indictment for the havoc Fitzgerald inflicted upon himself and his wife in Paris. Juxtaposed against the scene of inadvertent self-betrayal with which the story begins, that lame final paragraph, so suffused with self-pity and denial, offers the definitive expression of Charlie's blindness, his ultimate refusal to own up to his inner conflicts and his inevitable agency in the damage he has sustained. Fitzgerald enables us to see, through the geography of the narrative, the persistence of "that condition of utter irresponsibility" which is the essence of Charlie's problem. Belatedly Fitzgerald understood how he and Zelda had managed in Paris and elsewhere "to make nothing out of something." In 1930 he used that insight to reverse the process, miraculously extracting something wise and brilliant from the emotional debris of the 1920s. But the end of "Babylon" also prefigured, with ironic prescience, the loneliness and disappointment that would darken his final decade.

2.

As Hemingway revised "The Snows of Kilimanjaro" in early 1936, he found himself brooding upon the evidence of Fitzgerald's decline. With disgust he had read in *Esquire* a series of confessional essays by Fitzgerald (later published collectively in *The Crack-up* [1945]), and he began to imagine his former expatriate crony as the epitome of the broken writer he meant to portray in "Snows." His story even included a biting reference to "poor Scott Fitzgerald"—later changed to "poor Julian"—and his naive idealization of the rich: "He thought they were a special glamourous race and when he found they weren't it wrecked him just as much as any other thing that wrecked him" (53). Always the moralist despite himself, Hemingway composed "Snows" as an analysis of wreckage and self-ruin; privately he excoriated the "miserable" *Esquire* pieces and Fitzgerald's willingness to "whine in public," and while he conceded that it was "rotten to speak against Scott after all he had to go through," Hemingway complained that he had seen "the first part of it and it was all so avoidable and self imposed" (*Selected Letters* 437–38). He *had* seen "the first part of it" in Paris and Antibes, but what lay beneath Hemingway's angry fixation with Fitzgerald's dissolution was, of course, his own intense yet unacknowledged identification with his friend's "avoidable and self imposed" destruction. As "Snows" eloquently suggests, Hemingway already suspected that, like the pathetic writer in his story, "he had traded away what remained of his old life" (46). Within the African story about a dying writer's reflections, he embedded a secret narrative of deception and betrayal to explain—albeit obliquely—how he started down the path to self-ruin and lost "*the Paris that he cared about*" ("Snows" 52; unless otherwise indicated, emphasis in original).

In the six years since abandoning his Left Bank apartment in January 1930, Hemingway had bought a home in Key West, become an aficionado of big-game fishing, gone on safari in Africa, and published three new books, all of which drew criticism for their cynical self-indulgence.[7] His relationship with Pauline Pfeiffer—the romance that brought an end to "the first part of Paris" in 1926—had, apart from interludes of edgy domesticity, settled into a routine of evasion and deceit: Hemingway went off fishing for weeks at a time on the *Pilar* (ironically, his pet nickname for Pauline), and since 1932 he had been involved intermittently in a dalliance with a wealthy socialite named Jane Mason. The hardworking, winsome young man who achieved literary fame in Paris in the 1920s had become (in Jeffrey Meyers's formulation) the "swaggering hero" of the 1930s, swiftly evolving into the "drunken braggart" of the 1940s. Meyers suggestively remarks that "in the mid-1930s Hemingway ironically and irrationally began to blame Pauline, as Harry blamed Helen in 'The Snows of Kilimanjaro,' for the corrupting influence of her wealth" (70, 290). Hemingway perhaps felt the same sense of depletion he ascribed to the dying Harry: "He had had his life and it was over and then he went on living it again with different people and more money, with the best of the same places, and some new ones" ("Snows" 44). The appearance of Fitzgerald's *Crack-up* pieces only intensified the latent self-judgment that fueled "Snows." After seven years in Key West, Hemingway worried that, like Fitzgerald and like his own dying writer-hero, he had "destroyed his talent by not using it" (45). His new story, arguably the most daring he ever composed, probed his blackest anxieties to reckon the extent of his own dissolution. The story looked back, ruefully yet elliptically, to a turning point in his apprenticeship as an expatriate writer.

Hemingway inscribed the secret narrative of that epoch in the italicized flashbacks that represent Harry's *recherche du temps perdu*. These reconstructed moments or episodes comprise "the things that he had saved to write" (41), the stored materials that, as a result of the writer's gangrene and septicemia, would never become the stuff of literature except insofar as the metatextuality of "Snows" preserves them. The flashbacks unfold a panorama of scenes from places where Harry (and Hemingway himself) had lived or traveled—Turkey, the Austrian Vorarlberg, the Black Forest, a ranch in Wyoming. Taken together, they sketch the story of Harry's experiences in World War I and his glimpses of the ensuing conflict between the Greeks and the Turks; they tell of later skiing vacations, fishing trips, and cattle drives. They incorporate haunting images of the dead or the dying: Williamson, the officer disemboweled by a stick bomb and begging to be shot (53); the dead soldiers in Turkey wearing *"white ballet skirts and upturned shoes with pompons on them"* (48); the frozen, gnawed body of the old man killed by the *"half-wit chore boy"* (52) at the ranch. And the flashbacks return insistently, as critics have observed, to the enigmatic image of the snow, presaging the story's final, mystical turn toward the summit of Kilimanjaro (Oldsey 69–73). But embedded within the italicized passages lies a covert, fragmentary account of Harry's self-ruin, composed of glancing allusions to his formative experiences in Paris.

Hemingway suggests the geosymbolic importance of Paris early in "Snows" when Helen remarks about Harry's infected scratch: "You never would have gotten anything like this in Paris. You always said you loved Paris. We could have stayed in Paris or gone anywhere" ("Snows" 41). Putatively a beloved place in the geography of Harry's life, Paris represents safety and comfort, a refuge from misfortune and mortality. Inexplicably, however, Harry's own effort to recollect the city leads to an explosion of self-contempt:

> "Where did we stay in Paris?" he asked the woman who was sitting by him in a canvas chair, now, in Africa.
> "At the Crillon. You know that."
> "Why do I know that?"
> "That's where we always stayed."
> "No. Not always."
> "There and at the Pavillion [*sic*] Henri-Quatre in St. Germain. You said you loved it there."
> "Love is a dunghill," said Harry. "And I'm the cock that gets on it to crow." (43)

This cryptic exchange offers several clues to the secret story of Harry's relation to Paris. It resonates with other accusations about the corrupting effect of Helen's wealth by identifying two luxury hotels—one on the place de la Concorde and one in the suburb of St. Germain-en-Laye—as places where the couple "always stayed" in Paris. The flicker of disagreement ("No. Not

always.") moreover hints at the discrepancy between Helen's carefully idealized remembrance of the recent past and Harry's troubled recollection of
his early days in Paris. Her reference to the Pavillon Henri-Quatre elicits a
sudden virulence, apparently because the hotel evokes for Harry not luxurious pleasure but degraded desire, associated with waste and possible trans-
gression. His repugnant metaphor exposes a scornful self-contempt, rooted
in his unmistakable disgust with love, the "dunghill," and sexual conquest,
figured by the crowing cock—the latter reference slyly linking France itself
(through its insignia, *le coq gaulois*) with phallic hubris.

The notion that Harry associates Paris with duplicity as well as desire
becomes more apparent as he reflects on his various amours. He admits that
lies have made him "more successful with women than when he had told
them the truth" (44), and he wonders acerbically why "when[ever] he fell in
love with another woman, that woman should always have more money than
the last one?" (45). Contemplating his liaison with Helen within a history of
fractious relationships, he thinks to himself, "He had never quarrelled much
with this woman, while with the women that he loved he had quarrelled so
much they had finally, always, with the corrosion of the quarrelling, killed
what they had together. He had loved too much, demanded too much, and he
wore it all out" (48). This chain of reflection leads, with psychic inevitability,
to the flashback that constitutes the crux of his covert narrative. Here Harry
uncovers a primal scene of desire significantly associated with Paris, the scene
to which all of his other conquests have a secondary, mimetic relationship:

> *He thought about alone in Constantinople that time, having quar-*
> *relled in Paris before he had gone out. He had whored the whole time*
> *and then, when that was over, and he had failed to kill his loneliness,*
> *but only made it worse, he had written her, the first one, the one who*
> *left him, a letter telling her how he had never been able to kill it.*
>
> *How when he thought he saw her outside the Regence one time*
> *it made him go all faint and sick inside, and that he would follow a*
> *woman who looked like her in some way, along the Boulevard, afraid*
> *to see it was not she, afraid to lose the feeling it gave him. How every*
> *one he had slept with had only made him miss her more. How what she*
> *had done could never matter since he knew he could not cure himself of*
> *loving her. He wrote this letter at the Club, cold sober, and mailed it to*
> *New York asking her to write him at the office in Paris. (48)*

In this complex remembrance, the writer dying in Africa recalls his visit to
Constantinople (during the 1922 Greek-Turkish War) and the fateful letter

that he composed back in Paris *"at the Club."* Reconstructing the epistolary moment, he remembers the phantasmic, unnamed *"first one,"* standing outside the Café-Restaurant de la Régence (161, rue du Faubourg St. Honoré). His imperishable yet uncertain glimpse—*"he* thought *he saw her"* (emphasis added)—makes him feel *"all faint and sick inside";* distance and separation define his momentary gaze, for now, presumably, she is someone else's lover. Using the Proustian mode of habitual past action Harry recalls a bleak period in Paris when *"he would follow a woman who looked like her along the Boulevard,"* in a pattern of obsession confirming that the object of desire is always obscure, always displaced from its apparent incarnation, always quite literally disembodied. These other women are not the beloved but evoke by physical resemblance the *"feeling"* associated with her, the longing that ultimately has no proper object or embodiment. The unnamed first love occupies a totemic place in the writer's unconscious precisely because she was *"the one who left him,"* and who thereby remains an irrecoverable absence. Harry perceives the emotional and symbolic linkage between the original beloved and his subsequent liaisons (*"every one he had slept with had only made him miss her more"*). The loss of his first love has shaped the economy of desire: The more desperate his efforts to recover her symbolically on the plane of the erotic, the more intensely he experiences his own emptiness and loneliness. For Harry, love is figuratively a dunghill.

The remembered glimpse of the beloved *"outside the Regence"* thus triggers a crucial revelation about the pattern of emotional wreckage in Harry's life. This recollection of a primal scene of desire on the rue du Faubourg St. Honoré folds into Harry's memory of another epoch in Paris and his symbolic reciprocation of the abandonment he has experienced. For Harry frames the remembrance of *"the first one"* and *"what she had done"* with an oblique reference to her successor, the wife with whom he *"quarrelled in Paris before he had gone out."* He has *"whored the whole time"* in Turkey in 1922 ostensibly because of their quarrels but actually—as we learn—because he has never been able to *"kill his loneliness,"* the sense of solitude rooted in his originary rejection by the nameless beloved. Thus in Constantinople he picks up *"a girl,"* has dinner with her, and then abandons her for *"a hot Armenian slut,"* a *"smooth-bellied, big-breasted"* woman who needs *"no pillow under her buttocks"* (48). That is, he acts out his own rejection by picking up one woman and then leaving her to bed another, all the while betraying a third woman back in Paris—his wife, the unknowing object of his sexual revenge—to *"kill"* the feelings of rejection inflicted by a fourth woman, his first love.

This pattern of betrayal recurs when Harry returns to Paris and (from the masculine sanctuary of his "Club") writes a supplicating letter to his first love. He performs this act, significantly, in the context of his reunion with "*his wife that now he loved again, the quarrel all over, the madness all over*" (49). Feeling "*glad to be home*" from Constantinople and "*back at the apartment*"— apparently the apartment near the place Contrescarpe mentioned later—he receives a shock when a letter from his first love arrives "*on a platter one morning*" (49) among some mail from the office. Hemingway here stages a brief but profoundly revealing moment as Harry tries to cover his symbolic betrayal with an act of deception: "*When he saw the handwriting he went cold all over and tried to slip the letter underneath another. But his wife said, 'Who is that letter from, dear?' and that was the end of the beginning of that*" (49). Vaguely reminiscent of another Parisian scene of unsuccessful dissembling in Poe's "Purloined Letter," Hemingway likewise emphasizes the repetition compulsion inherent in an effort to conceal the sign of secret desire. For although Harry tries to slide the telltale letter from "*the first one*" under another envelope, he cannot repress or conceal his longing for her, nor can he apparently escape the repetition mechanism that causes him to reenact his initial abandonment by betraying the beloved's successor. Indeed, the purely symbolic infidelity enacted here seems finally a trope for later acts of deception, including (presumably) the relationship with Helen associated with the Crillon and the Pavillon Henri-Quatre. Harry's terse final comment, "*that was the end of the beginning of that*," seems to signal the impending breakup of the marriage, as if the letter, the sign of a hitherto hidden and obsessive relation, had inevitably set in motion a chain of subsequent betrayals. And in a sense it has. But the reversal of the anticipated word order—we expect him to say "that was the beginning of the end" of their marriage—carries another implication, one having to do as much with the beginning of Harry's relationship to Paris as with his abandonment of the wife he "*loved again*" back in the apartment near the place Contrescarpe.

In the convoluted unfolding of Harry's secret story, his narrative of self-ruin, the next flashback culminates in a significant four-paragraph reconstruction of his memories of the working-class neighborhood on the Left Bank near the Panthéon. Sweat, poverty, and drunkenness typify the *quartier* around the Café des Amateurs, an area that stands in marked contrast to the milieu of luxury that Harry and Helen have subsequently inhabited. Hemingway remarks that Harry "*knew his neighbors in that quarter then because they all were poor*" (51). Oddly, however, the remembrance avoids any reference to the "wife" associated with the events of 1922. Instead, she disappears into the pronoun "*they*," as when the flashback mentions "*the Bal Musette they lived above.*" But in two oblique ways Hemingway suggests Harry's subliminal remorse about the way he destroyed his marriage. First, the flashback betrays an insistent interest in relations between husbands and wives, with Harry recalling "*the locataire across the hall whose husband was a bicycle racer*," "*the*

husband of the woman who ran the Bal Musette" (51), and finally Marie, the
femme de ménage who explains that her husband's shorter working days will
mean more drinking: "*It is the wife of the working man who suffers from this
shortening of hours*" (52).

Another reflection of Harry's repressed feelings about his former wife
inheres in the sense of loss evoked by the old neighborhood. With palpable
regret, Harry recognizes that "*he had never written about Paris. Not the Paris
that he cared about*" (52). The Paris that he cherishes is precisely the shabby
place Contrescarpe *quartier* of 1922, linked explicitly to the origin of his literary career and tacitly to the wife whom he loved despite the quarrels. In effect
he projects his attachment to her into the particulars of place:

> *And in that poverty, and in that quarter across the street from a Boucherie
> Chevaline and a wine co-operative he had written the start of all he was
> to do. There never was another part of Paris that he loved like that, the
> sprawling trees, the old white plastered houses painted brown below, the
> long green of the autobus in that round square, the purple flower dye upon
> the paving, the sudden drop down the hill of the rue Cardinal Lemoine
> to the River, and the other way the narrow crowded world of the rue
> Mouffetard. (51)*

Noting that "*there were only two rooms in the apartments where they lived*,"
Harry again avoids mentioning his wife. Through an act of desperation,
signaled by the arrival of the letter, he has betrayed her; now, perhaps to
avoid the pain of remorse, he denies her very place in that world, figuring
her only as a shadowy absence, a pronominal trace. By metonymic substitu-
tion, however, the old neighborhood becomes the site and symbol of Harry's
longing for the irrecoverable: for youth, for his literary beginnings, for the
self that he once was, and for the spouse whom he loved. His comment
about locale—"*there never was another part of Paris that he loved like that*"—
implicitly distinguishes his wife from the other lovers he has known there.
Hemingway suggests that Paris has been the essential scene of Harry's erotic
life; it has witnessed the various stages of his metamorphosis from wounded
lover, to unfaithful husband, to cynical rake. From the experience of loss
on the rue du Faubourg St. Honoré to the dunghill of desire at the Pavillon
Henri-Quatre, the dying Harry now understands the phases of his life in
relation to the city he has loved, the place where he has "*written the start of all
he was to do*." Yet that implicitly epochal event—the arrival of the letter—has
marked "*the end of the beginning*" (49) of his career and of his relation to the
Paris he loves. He has forfeited that best of all possible worlds because he
"*loved too much, demanded too much*," because he could not surmount the pain

of losing *the first one* (48). To relieve his *"hollow sick"* loneliness, he has cast off his wife and inflicted upon himself a perverse self-punishment: He falls prey to Helen, to the charms of wealth and indolence, and thereby destroys his marriage, his connections with working-class Paris, and eventually his discipline as a writer. Only belatedly, as a dying man on an African plain performing the final audit of his earthly account, does he recognize the damage he has done and the irretrievability of all that he has lost.

By 1936 Hemingway had achieved enough distance from his Paris years to survey the personal wreckage caused by his own destructive decisions and impulsive *liaisons dangereuses*. Although he rose from obscurity to renown and fashioned (in Archibald MacLeish's phrase) "a style for his time" on the Left Bank, the city's sensual, epicurean value system affected him profoundly, fostering a brooding awareness that "nothing was simple there" (*Feast* 58). Virtually from his arrival, Hemingway experienced moral ambivalence: He jeered at the "inmates" frequenting the Café Rotonde, then himself became a confirmed Bohemian who (in Bill Gorton's phrase) liked to "hang around cafés"; he learned to write "true sentences" from mentors like Anderson and Stein and then brusquely repudiated them, denying their influence; and in letters he flaunted his conjugal bliss with Hadley while becoming increasingly obsessed with unconventional sexual practices (Reynolds 24–25, 34). In the same neighborhood recollected by the dying writer in "Snows," he watched prostitutes plying their trade at the dance hall they lived above, and he discovered at the nearby Bal de la Montagne Sainte-Geneviève the spectacle of same-sex dancing and cross-dressing. At the cafés he met gay and lesbian couples (such as Jane Heap and Margaret Anderson), encountered intriguing bisexuals like Djuna Barnes, followed the semipublic affairs of Ezra Pound and Ford Madox Ford, and heard about the Montparnasse fad of group sex "sandwiching."

Although Hemingway went to Paris partly to escape the straight-laced moralism personified by his mother, Grace Hall Hemingway, he remained decidedly conventional—"ninety per cent Rotarian," as Stein calculated—at least until early 1924, when he and Hadley (possibly in reaction to recent parenthood) decided to plunge into the new hedonism of the postwar era: "We lived like savages and kept our own tribal rules and had our own customs and our own standards, secrets, taboos, and delights" ("As long as I ..." 4).[8] The couple cultivated same-sex hairstyles, wore matching clothing, and fantasized about switching genders. The innocuous sexual game-playing hinted, however, at problems in their relationship. Hemingway's increasing restlessness led in 1925 to a tantalizing flirtation with Duff Twysden (the prototype of Brett Ashley) and soon thereafter to a steamy romance with Pauline Pfeiffer, an affair intermittently conducted (as *A Moveable Feast* implies) as a virtual ménage à trois. The break with Hadley, which occurred in 1926, marked the definitive end of an epoch—"the early days when we were very poor and very happy" (*Moveable Feast* 211). As his memoir suggests, nothing would ever seem simple or innocent again.

Why a writer so guarded as Hemingway saw fit to reconstruct his private history in "Snows" is an intriguing question. Transparently, Harry's tortured recollection of "*the first one*" and the arrival of the incriminating letter amounts to a veiled rationalization for the breakup of Hemingway's first marriage. The biographical subtext becomes more profoundly suggestive when we note that Hemingway exchanged letters in late 1922—more than a year after his marriage to Hadley—with Agnes von Kurowsky, the Red Cross nurse with whom he fell in love in Italy in 1918. His urge to contact her suggests that he had not entirely recovered from the emotional wound inflicted in March 1919 by the "dear John" letter describing her engagement to an Italian officer. Possibly, like his fictional protagonist, he wrote to Agnes from the Anglo-American Press Club just after his return from Constantinople—a junket that had occasioned a bitter quarrel with Hadley. The reply from Agnes reached him, however, not in Paris but in Chamby, Switzerland, where Hemingway was skiing with his wife in early 1923 during the holiday season. While there is no evidence that the young reporter had a heartbreaking glimpse of Agnes on the streets of Paris, her December 1922 letter may provide the origin of that imaginary scene:

> . . . sometimes I get lonesome, and then . . . I dream of Paris—that dear old place, where I had so much time on my hands, and roamed about in so many funny places. If I could only stand just now—at early twilight—at the Place de la Concorde, and see the little taxis spinning around those corners, & the soft lights, & the Tuileries fountain—oh, my, I'm homesick for the smell of chestnuts on a grey, damp Fall day—for Pruniers, the Savoia (Noel Peters) and my pet little restaurant behind the Madelaine [*sic*]—Bernard's, where I ate crème chocolate every night. Maybe I'd better stop, or the paper will get soft & blurry out of sympathy for my sorrows. (von Kurowsky 166–67)

Between Red Cross service missions, Agnes had spent four months in Paris from October 1920 until February 1921. Depicting herself provocatively with "so much time on [her] hands," Agnes mentions being most recently in the city "a year ago this Nov."—barely a month prior to the arrival of the newlyweds, Ernest and Hadley, in December 1921. By a few weeks, that is, Hemingway had missed a chance reunion with Agnes at Prunier's, or the

Savoia (also known as Noël Peters's) or Bernard's—restaurants all located roughly in the same Right Bank *quartier* where he installed himself in early 1922 as a regular at the Anglo-American Press Club. The thought of that missed encounter with his first love must have tormented him: Soon thereafter he wrote "A Very Short Story," the first literary evidence of the persistent fantasizing about Agnes that culminated in *A Farewell to Arms*. Harry's recollection in "Snows" of the letter to his lost love extends that preoccupation into the mid-1930s, and the imagined glimpse of *"the first one"* outside the Régence marks a revealing excavation from the writerly unconscious: Hemingway apparently reached back almost fifteen years to resurrect—*from a letter he still preserved*—the image of Agnes von Kurowsky emerging from a Right Bank restaurant "on a grey, damp Fall day" in November 1921.

If so, Hemingway's own remembrance of things past—as figured in "Snows"—contains an important insight into the fate of his first marriage. It implies his realization that the end of his marriage began in 1922 with an act of infidelity: Not the "whoring" in Constantinople that Hemingway later confessed was his only sexual betrayal of Hadley until the affair with Pauline (Kert 125), but rather the letter to Agnes that implicitly indicated his fixation with her. Although Hemingway had told Hadley about his wartime romance and somewhat perversely visited with her the Italian settings associated with that relationship, the unexpected arrival of the letter from Agnes in response to his own may have heightened the marital tensions provoked by Hadley's loss of Hemingway's manuscripts a few weeks earlier.[9] Despite its decorous, friendly tone, the communication from Agnes would have exposed the hitherto secret letter from Ernest, allowing Hadley to glimpse both his continuing obsession with Agnes and his propensity for duplicity. And indeed Hemingway's fictional reference to an awkward scene of discovery—shifted from Chamby to Paris—hints that Hadley did see the letter. The author figures the moment as the incipient yet irreversible breakdown of marital trust, the prelude to an unspecified later episode in Harry's amatory career that brought actual separation and divorce. Yet the coded narrative in "Snows" may also be seen as a disguised (and equivocal) apology to Hadley. By representing Harry's betrayal as a symptom of compulsive desire, his inability to "kill the loneliness" inflicted by his first love's rejection, Hemingway was implicitly rationalizing his abandonment of Hadley, even as he intimated his residual feelings for her in Harry's plangent remembrance of the old apartment and "the Paris he cared about."

By ridiculing the *Crack-up* essays and the "shamelessness of defeat" epitomized by Fitzgerald, Hemingway attempted in 1936 to displace his own sense of failure and wasted opportunity. But the embedded story in "Snows" conveys an unsparing indictment of himself for damage inflicted upon Hadley—and ultimately upon himself as a writer—during the "nightmare winter" of 1925–1926 and the "murderous summer that was to follow" (*Moveable Feast* 207). The need to recover and celebrate the "magic" life destroyed during that period of upheaval haunted Hemingway to the end of his days. Among other tasks, *A Moveable Feast* makes restitution to Hadley by idealizing her and restoring her to that "cheerful, gay flat" near the place Contrescarpe. It reconstructs in all of its luminous particularity "the first part of Paris" whose traumatic loss he had figured in the cryptic story concealed two decades earlier in "Snows." Hemingway's repositioning of Hadley within the memoir of those early years reverses the narrative gesture by which he repressed her presence in the African story of 1936.

3.

"Babylon Revisited" and "The Snows of Kilimanjaro" thus reflect on each author's missteps in Paris during the Jazz Age. From the more somber Zeitgeist of the 1930s, Fitzgerald and Hemingway produced fictions calculated, on one level, to evoke sympathy for the male protagonists with whom they so obviously identified. But in a move that reveals their maturation since the "crazy years," both ultimately resisted the impulse to self-pity and subjected their fictional doubles to unsparing scrutiny, dramatizing the remorse and self-questioning—the deepening of moral insight—that represents perhaps the most significant literary consequence of the personal wreckage they sustained abroad. Their determination to revisit the ruins of their own youthful marriages and early careers, to contemplate again (admittedly, with minor evasions and equivocations) the heedless acts and bad decisions of the 1920s, corroborates Faulkner's famous declaration that "the problems of the human heart in conflict with itself . . . alone can make good writing because only that is worth writing about" (3). "Babylon" and "Snows" each bear witness to a lacerating conflict between an older, authorial self and a younger, experiential self—between a judgmental and thus patently American self and an insouciant, expatriate self.

Although their paths subsequently diverged, Fitzgerald and Hemingway shared the life of literary exile and—somewhat to their mutual chagrin—discovered themselves linked in the public mind (thanks to Stein's quip) as leaders of the "lost generation." The uneasy friendship that began in the Dingo Bar in 1925 underwent numerous reversals, permutations, and estrangements during the fifteen years that it endured. After the summer of 1929—the last season of their expatriate camaraderie in Paris—Fitzgerald felt that he could no longer assume with Hemingway a relationship of literary equality and common respect. Writing in his Notebooks, he remarked: "I talk with the authority of failure—Ernest with the authority of success. We could never sit across the same table again" (Wilson 181).

For Fitzgerald, the past was prologue to an even more difficult decade. When he returned from Europe in 1931, facing the nightmare of Zelda's illness and the ordeal of completing *Tender Is the Night*, he gave up the fantasy of recovering a glamorous expatriate life. Though he contemplated a transatlantic journey in the summer of 1932, the plan never materialized, and over the next few years Fitzgerald's own reduced circumstances made European travel increasingly unthinkable. Like Dick Diver, Fitzgerald had suffered a "lesion of vitality" in Europe, and he struggled unsuccessfully during the last nine years of his life to recover the imaginative facility of his pre-exilic years. Although he managed to finish his novel (remaining tormented, to the end, by its imperfections), the chaos of his personal life before and after the "crackup" of 1935 greatly debilitated him as a writer. In the mid-1930s he conjured up a series of lame, romantic tales about a medieval French knight named Philippe, thus perhaps assuaging his memory of expatriate disasters with a dream of Gallic heroism, projected onto a character curiously reminiscent of Hemingway. Fitzgerald's work in Hollywood in the late 1930s led to a film script based on "Babylon Revisited," but in that screenplay, entitled "Cosmopolitan," Paris represents little more than a flimsy backdrop for the drastically revised, melodramatic action. In producing that treatment—as Matthew J. Bruccoli notes—Fitzgerald "removed the *revisited* theme" (*Babylon Revisited: The Screenplay* 189). There was no going back: even the Paris of memory had become irrecoverable.

Hemingway likewise returned from Europe deeply changed, though the nature of his transformation was less apparent. In the 1930s he demonstrated a deepening cynicism (flaunted in "A Natural History of the Dead"), a greater callousness in personal relationships, and a new preoccupation with self-indulgent travel journalism. After the earlier achievement of *The Sun Also Rises* (1926) and *A Farewell to Arms* (1929), his only novel of the decade, *To Have and Have Not* (1937), reflected a palpable decline in creative power, and his stories of the period were notoriously uneven in quality (Lynn 409–10). His sense of decline as an author may underlie the crisis—not to say the "crack-up"—that he suffered in August 1936 (the same month that "Snows" appeared in *Esquire*), when he confessed to Marjorie Kinnan Rawlings, "Lately I have felt I was going to die in a short time" (*Selected Letters* 449). The same month he jested with Archibald MacLeish: "Me I like life very much. So much it will be a big disgust when [I] have to shoot myself" (*Selected Letters* 453). Hemingway postponed his fatal disgust another twenty-five years, however, outliving Fitzgerald and returning repeatedly to Paris. He sojourned there several times during the 1930s and helped to liberate "Paname" from Nazi occupation in 1944; he embarked in the postwar years on a trilogy of ultimately posthumous works (*Islands in the Stream*, *The Garden of Eden*, and

A Moveable Feast) testifying to the deep and lasting influence of the early years that he spent in France. In *A Moveable Feast* Hemingway's fetishizing of certain elements of his life there—the old apartment, his dinners with Hadley, the Luxembourg gardens, Sylvia Beach's bookstore, the racetracks and the velodrome—reflects more than nostalgia; it betrays a complex, tragic awareness that what he had gained and lost then had been elemental, essential, and irreplaceable.

Reckoning the effects of the Paris years in "Babylon" and "Snows," Fitzgerald and Hemingway implicitly raised intricate questions about the city's influence on their own lives and writings. As noted earlier, their shared emphasis on emotional wreckage implicitly challenges extant studies celebrating exile in France unproblematically as boon and privilege. It would be reductive, of course, to attribute each writer's problems during the 1930s to the excesses of expatriate life in the 1920s, for many other factors affected their personal and professional vicissitudes. But it would be equally naive to assume that the consequences of living abroad had been uniformly propitious.

Decades ago, Malcolm Cowley discussed the "deracination" of his generation, the way that it had been "wrenched away from [an] attachment to any region or tradition" (9, 27–48). Fitzgerald and Hemingway initially reveled in their uprooting. Freed from American mores and family influences, inhabiting a culture more tolerant of vice and pleasure than our own, *both* writers indulged in "secrets, taboos, and delights," revolted against middle-class conventions, and managed to smash apart their personal lives. With palpable regret, both belatedly recognized (and dramatized in fiction) the results of their recklessness. Far from their native shores, released from any attachment to "region or tradition," they explored in Paris the beguiling possibilities of an expatriate life predicated on the desire—the ineluctable "hunger" metaphorized in Hemingway's memoir—that always culminates in the present moment.

But in that foreign place, neither writer could escape the weight of time, the inevitability of consequence, or the burden of memory. The retrospective vision of "Babylon" and "Snows" imposes a sense of fate and history upon the geography of exile. Facing different kinds of adversity in the 1930s, Fitzgerald and Hemingway reached similar conclusions about their experiences in France. Those passionate years had seemed truly "magic," and Paris, the site of the Modern and the source of the New, the place (in Stein's phrase) "where the twentieth century was," seemed a locus of unconstrained pleasure and creativity. But as Hemingway later perceived, Paris was also "a very old city" where everything was "more complicated" than it first appeared (*Moveable Feast* 119), and where young American writers hell-bent on fame could succumb to their own illusions of greatness and indestructibility, make irreversible mistakes, and lose the very things they cared about most. Eventually, however, the disasters of the 1920s produced moral insight: Not until they had fallen, failed, and experienced irrevocable losses could Fitzgerald and Hemingway confront the potential delusions of literary exile and write the enduring stories of the 1930s that calculated the possible personal costs of the expatriate's "swell life."

NOTES

1. Writing to Maxwell Perkins about a review of *The Sun Also Rises*, Hemingway observed: "It was refreshing to see someone have some doubts that I took the Gertrude Stein thing very seriously—I meant to play off against that splendid bombast (Gertrude's assumption of prophetic roles)" (*Selected Letters* 229). Matthew J. Bruccoli counts Stein among several literary friends with whom Hemingway eventually broke, noting that he had "a compulsion to declare his independence from, or non-indebtedness to, writers who could be said to have helped or influenced him" (*Fitzgerald and Hemingway* 4).

2. Though he mocked Stein's characterization of his generation, Hemingway acknowledged in a letter to his mother that he meant to portray the expatriates as "burned out, hollow and smashed" (*Selected Letters* 243). Hemingway's explanations to his mother should not be accepted uncritically, but there is corroborating evidence in his comments to Maxwell Perkins that he felt "a great deal of fondness and admiration for the [abiding] earth and *not a hell of a lot for my generation*" (*Selected Letters* 229; emphasis added). About his waning enthusiasm for life on the Left Bank, Hemingway remarked in a letter to Jane Heap in August, 1925: "Paris is getting shot to hell. Not like the old days."

3. Fitzgerald's account of the taxi ride, as published, will perplex anyone familiar with the geography of Paris: en route to the Peters's residence, Charlie crosses the Seine into the Left Bank, then recrosses the river to the avenue de l'Opéra on the Right Bank before finally returning to the Left Bank. As Garry N. Murphy and William C. Slattery have shown, Fitzgerald intended to delete the paragraph referring to the Boulevard des Capucines and the place de la Concorde.

4. Fitzgerald made this connection even more apparent in his revision of "Babylon" as the screenplay "Cosmopolitan" in 1940. His hero, Charles Wales, has just decided to give up a fabulous career as a Wall Street trader when the action begins; en route to Europe, while Charles is negotiating a deal in the ship's Brokerage Office, his wife commits suicide by jumping into the ocean. See *Babylon Revisited: The Screenplay*.

5. This is very nearly the imagery used by Malcolm Cowley in *Exile's Return*, one of the earliest and best accounts of the American expatriate movement of the twenties. For Cowley, France was the "Holy Land" where literary gods like Flaubert might be propitiated (102–3).

6. The Empire and the Casino de Paris are listed together under "Music Halls" in the Baedeker guide, *Paris and Its Environs* (34). It is worth noting that the music hall listed just ahead of the Empire was the Olympia (28, boulevard des Capucines), where Zelda took ballet lessons in an upstairs apartment in 1929.

7. Both *Death in the Afternoon* (1932) and *Green Hills of Africa* (1934) contained potshots at literary contemporaries as well as at irritating critics. *Winner Take Nothing* (1933) included some great stories (like "A Way You'll Never Be," "A Clean, Well-Lighted Place," and "Hills Like White Elephants") but also some of Hemingway's laziest work. Kenneth S. Lynn remarks, "Nothing that Fitzgerald ever peddled to a slick-paper publication was shoddier than 'One Reader Writes' or 'A Day's Wait'" (410).

8. In *Imagining Paris* (134–39) I discuss this tantalizing fragment in detail.

9. This well-known episode—recounted memorably in *A Moveable Feast* (73–75) and fictionalized in *The Garden of Eden* as well as the narrative published as "The Strange Country"—apparently contributed to the "friction" that developed between Ernest and Hadley from late 1922 on.

Works Cited

Baedeker, Karl. *Paris and Its Environs: With Routes From London to Paris—Handbook for Travellers.* 19th rev. ed. Leipzig: Karl Baedeker, 1924.

Baker, Carlos. "When the Story Ends: 'Babylon Revisited.'" *The Short Stories of F. Scott Fitzgerald: New Approaches in Criticism.* Ed. Jackson R. Bryer. Madison: U of Wisconsin P, 1982. 269–77.

Benstock, Shari. *Women of the Left Bank: Paris, 1900–1940.* Austin: U of Texas P, 1986.

Bruccoli, Matthew J. *Fitzgerald and Hemingway: A Dangerous Friendship.* New York: Carroll & Graf, 1994.

———. *Some Sort of Epic Grandeur: The Life of F. Scott Fitzgerald.* San Diego: Harcourt Brace Jovanovich, 1981.

Carpenter, Humphrey. *Geniuses Together: American Writers in Paris in the 1920s.* Boston: Houghton Mifflin, 1988.

Cowley, Malcolm. *Exile's Return: A Literary Odyssey of the 1920s.* 1932. New York: Penguin, 1976.

Faulkner, William. "Nobel Prize Address." *The Faulkner Reader.* New York: Modern Library, 1961. 3–4.

Fitzgerald, F. Scott. "Babylon Revisited." *The Short Stories of F. Scott Fitzgerald: A New Collection.* Ed. Matthew J. Bruccoli. New York: Scribners, 1989. 616–33.

———. *Babylon Revisited: The Screenplay.* Intro. Budd Schulberg. New York: Carroll and Graf, 1993.

———. *F. Scott Fitzgerald's Ledger: A Facsimile.* Washington, DC: NCR/Microcard Editions, 1972.

———. *The Letters of F. Scott Fitzgerald.* Ed. Andrew Turnbull. New York: Scribners, 1963.

———. *A Life in Letters.* Ed. Matthew J. Bruccoli, with the assistance of Judith S. Baughman. New York: Scribners, 1994.

———. *Tender Is the Night.* New York: Scribners, 1934.

Ford, Hugh. *Published in Paris: American and British Writers, Printers, and Publishers in Paris, 1920–39.* Yonkers, NY: Pushcart P, 1975.

Hemingway, Ernest. "As long as I did newspaper work. . . ." Unpublished. Item 526. Hemingway Collection. John F. Kennedy Library, Boston.

———. *Ernest Hemingway: Selected Letters, 1917–1961.* Ed. Carlos Baker. New York: Scribners, 1981.

———. Letter to Jane Heap, ca. August 25, 1925. Unpublished. *Little Review* Collection. University of Wisconsin–Milwaukee Library, Milwaukee, WI.

————. *A Moveable Feast*. New York: Scribners, 1964.

————. "The Snows of Kilimanjaro." *The Complete Short Stories of Ernest Hemingway*. New York: Scribners, 1987. 39–56.

————. *The Sun Also Rises*. New York: Scribners, 1926.

Kennedy, J. Gerald. *Imagining Paris: Exile, Writing, and American Identity*. New Haven CT: Yale UP, 1993.

Kert, Bernice. *The Hemingway Women: Those Who Loved Him—The Wives and Others*. New York: Norton, 1983.

Lynn, Kenneth S. *Hemingway*. New York: Simon and Schuster, 1987.

Meyers, Jeffrey. *Hemingway: A Biography*. New York: Harper & Row, 1985.

Murphy, Garry N., and William C. Slattery. "The Flawed Text of 'Babylon Revisited': A Challenge to Editors, a Warning to Readers." *Studies in Short Fiction* 18 (1981): 315–18.

Oldsey, Bern. "The Snows of Ernest Hemingway." *Ernest Hemingway: A Collection of Criticism*. Ed. Arthur Waldhorn. New York: McGraw-Hill, 1973. 56–82.

Pizer, Donald. *American Expatriate Writing and the Paris Moment: Modernism and Place*. Baton Rouge: Louisiana State UP, 1995.

Reynolds, Michael. *Hemingway: The Paris Years*. Cambridge, MA: Blackwell, 1989.

Twitchell, James B. "'Babylon Revisited': Chronology and Characters." *Fitzgerald/Hemingway Annual 1978*: 155–60.

von Kurowsky, Agnes. *Hemingway in Love and War: The Lost Diary of Agnes Von Kurowsky, Her Letters and the Correspondence of Ernest Hemingway*. Ed. Henry Serrano Villard and James Nagel. Boston: Northeastern UP, 1989.

Wickes, George. *Americans in Paris*. 1969. New York: Da Capo, 1980.

Wilson, Edmund, ed. *The Crack-up*. New York: New Directions, 1945.

RICHARD ALLAN DAVISON

Art and Autobiography in Fitzgerald's "Babylon Revisited"

"Babylon Revisited" is F. Scott Fitzgerald's most acclaimed short story. That it is also one of his best is due to his brilliant stylistic and structural control[1] and the haunting complexity of the main character, Charlie Wales, alias Charles J. Wales of Prague. In his creation of a character whose ambivalences encompass hope, courage, nostalgia, anger, restraint, self-pity, pathos, regeneration, resignation, and self-destructive tragedy—virtually everything but humor—Fitzgerald has drawn more heavily from his own life experiences than critics have acknowledged. Fitzgerald's letters and essays about an analogous period in his life reflect his own agonized mind and demonstrate his deep sympathy for Wales, who is, more than most of Fitzgerald's characters, his alter ego. A 1979 interview with Fitzgerald's daughter, Scottie Fitzgerald Smith, and new information from one of Scottie's childhood friends and playmates reinforce these strong autobiographical overtones and undercurrents in "Babylon Revisited."

In her 1982 memoir, the daughter of Fitzgerald's friends Gerald and Sara Murphy, Honoria Murphy Donnelly, recalled:

> Mother expressed her discomfort at being subjected to Scott's "analysis, subanalysis, and criticism," which she found "on the whole unfriendly." The purpose of Scott's scrutiny, she soon realized, was

From *F. Scott Fitzgerald: New Perspectives*, edited by Jackson R. Bryer, Alan Margolies, and Ruth Prigozy, pp. 192–202. Copyright © 2000 by the University of Georgia Press.

to gather material for characterizations in his writing, which in my parents' case appeared in *Tender Is the Night*. Mother resented being used in such a way. No matter how fond she was of Scott—and her affection for both Scott and Zelda was very genuine—she believed that her privacy had been violated.

I too was a subject of Scott's analytical approach. I was only eight in the summer of 1926, but I well remember him as a man, very handsome in a delicate way, who would stare at me and ask penetrating questions. Why, he insisted on knowing, did I like the color red. Because my dress is red, or because I like the pink and red flowers in the garden, I would reply in my struggling way. I later became aware, as Mother had, that Scott had studied me for the purpose of fictional character depictions. The little girl in *Babylon Revisited* [*sic*] is probably more Scottie Fitzgerald than I, but it is not insignificant that he named her Honoria.[2]

A year later in an October 16, 1983, letter to me that accompanied her annotated copy of "Babylon Revisited," Honoria Murphy Donnelly cited more specific parallels: "the role playing game they [Charlie and his daughter Honoria] have is rather like Scottie as a child." The annotations argue for a pastiche of autobiographical echoes in "Babylon Revisited": "I didn't act demonstrative[ly] ... as a child ... Scottie [unlike Honoria Murphy, but like Honoria Wales] call[ed] her father 'Daddy.'" "Both Scott and my father [like Charlie to the fictional Honoria] were warm to us." "[R]ole playing [like Honoria Wales's] was typical of Scottie when she was young ... I recall with great pleasure what fun it was to play with her." "Scott had a collection of lead soldiers [like those Charlie gives to the Peterses]." In the side margin next to Charlie's and Honoria's discussion of lunch opening section 2, Donnelly wrote: "This is a conversation that could conceivably have come up with *either* Fitz's or Murphys." And in the side margin next to Lincoln Peters's "You children go in and start your soup,"[3] she added: "Murphys maybe[;] both families kept a strict food schedule for our own good." Her letter and annotations (which Eleanor Lanahan's new biography of Scottie corroborates)[4] make clear her belief that much of Fitzgerald's story is a blend of biographical data from both the Fitzgeralds and the Murphys.

With a rare creative blending Fitzgerald has crafted in "Babylon Revisited" the life models of himself, Zelda, Scottie, Honoria Murphy, Aunt Rosalind, and Uncle Newman (Zelda's sister and brother-in-law) into redoubtable actors in a trial for which the reader must share the agonies as both judge and jury. The emotional lives of both Wales and Fitzgerald stand as defendants. It is a shattering ordeal for all. Almost masochistically, Fitzgerald has placed

Wales in an atmosphere of an impending doom, a doom as inevitable as that of Stephen Crane's Swede in "The Blue Hotel." He has adroitly manipulated most readers into both liking and sympathizing with Charlie while suggesting at the very outset that Charlie will, at least temporarily, fail in his battle for his daughter Honoria, fail in his attempt to recapture his daughter, if not his honor.

Charlie would like custody of this child he is in Paris to regain, and in many ways he deserves to have Honoria back, to spirit her away to be the daughter of his current self, the financially secure and respected Charles J. Wales of Prague. What is even clearer is Honoria's strong desire to be with her father. Honoria throws herself joyfully and lovingly into his arms. She asks him, without prompting, when she will be coming to live with him. She reveals her qualified regard for Marion Peters, her maternal aunt and (with Lincoln Peters) dutiful guardian. It becomes apparent in her initial refusal of Charlie's offer of expensive gifts that love for her father transcends that of material goods. Charlie, not surprisingly for a father who has not seen his daughter in ten months, brings Honoria a doll at their first meeting at the Peterses. The next day, over lunch, however, he raises the ante, announcing to her: "First we're going to the toy store in the Rue Saint-Honoré and buy you anything you like. And then we're going to the vaudeville at the Empire" (307). Honoria answers: "I like it about the vaudeville, but not the toy store" (307). She appreciates that she already "had lots of things" and, worried that they are not "rich anymore" and wanting him more than his possessions, only reluctantly and "resignedly" (307) agrees to accept his offer of more material gifts.

Charlie's love for Honoria is equally clear. Charlie continually refuses that second drink. It is evident that he is deeply disturbed by Duncan Schaeffer's and Lorraine Quarrles's "unwelcome" intrusion into the loving intimacy of his luncheon with Honoria and horrified by their drunken disruption of his quiet triumph at the Peterses' apartment, where, for a time, victory in the quest for Honoria seems his. Charlie, then, would like very much to have Honoria, and Fitzgerald prompts most readers to sympathize with his desire.

Yet as several critics have argued so forcefully, Charlie's ambivalent urges and his persistent need for self-justification tend to undermine his good intentions.[5] His reluctance to accept his share of the blame for the destructive period in his past that placed Honoria in the custody of the Peterses, himself in a sanitarium and his wife, Helen, in an early grave, undercuts his apparent reformation. Charlie nowhere acknowledges that he was partly to blame for Helen's death. This reluctance to accept proper responsibility for his faults and make full atonement for them is apparent in most of what he says and does. Why else does he long so for echoes of his turbulent past—the tempting cafés, the nostalgic music, the colored lights, the names of discredited friends who shared them? Why does he make his nostalgic journey through the streets of Paris?[6] Why does he insist upon that one drink a day? (Isn't it an unnecessary temptation much like that of the quart bottle of whiskey Doc keeps in the kitchen cabinet in William Inge's play *Come Back, Little Sheba*?[7]) And why does Charlie at the very beginning of the story plant the seed of his own destruction by leaving the Peterses' address with the Ritz barman after inquiring about former acquaintances, willing accomplices from his period of dissipation? Why, in a word, is he at the Ritz bar at all? If he is attempting to demonstrate his triumph over past weaknesses, trying to prove to himself that they cannot engulf him, it is a questionable attempt at best. For the story begins and ends with Charlie at the scene of his most reprehensible moments, in an atmosphere as precarious as that of Hemingway's "The Sea Change." In Hemingway's story (also published in 1931), the main character, stunned by the departure of his girlfriend, who has abandoned him for a lesbian affair, is left drinking in the company of an accommodating bartender and what a 1930s audience would view as effete homosexuals. Charlie's bartender is equally accommodating in a bar that is almost empty but for "a group of strident queens" Charlie watches "installing themselves in a corner" (303). Although Charlie waves away the bartender's offer of a second drink (and everyone else's for that matter), his psychological state at the story's end is, like Phil's at the end of Hemingway's story, one of stunned desperation.

A more positive reading of Wales's scribbling of Lincoln Peters's address for the barman at the beginning of "Babylon Revisited" might include self-punishment, the threshold to his admission of guilt.[8] The act is much like Silas Lapham's "accidental" burning of his new house, which, as partial atonement for his own guilt, does lead to Lapham's moral rise and redemptive sacrificial act. Charles does not progress this far. There is a deeper desperation in his need for Honoria. He deems it necessary to buy her expensive presents. There is desperation and pathos in his dreamlike return to his dead wife, who is first envisioned in a white dress, as if in willful contrast to Marion's funereal black. Fitzgerald points up this contrast in his revisions of the magazine version of "Babylon Revisited" by making Marion a more formidable and somewhat more domestic opponent to Charlie, which makes clearer her ability to take adequate care of Honoria. Instead of *"fiddling"* with "the *glass grapes* on her necklace,"[9] Marion *"plays"* "with the *black stars* on her necklace" (*Reader* 311; emphasis added), suggesting a more potent control over Charlie's destiny. Instead of sitting "behind empty coffee cups" (*Post* 82) she sits "behind the coffee service" (*Reader* 311), suggesting a firmer control over her household. Instead of coming "back into the little salon" (*Post* 4) she comes "back from the kitchen" (*Reader* 305), suggesting a more intimate involvement with the day-to-day rituals affecting Honoria's life with the Peterses. In "half sleep" Charlie also sees the deceased Helen in a swing that moves faster and faster, blurring the past, present, and future as well as merging them.[10] At the end of the story he assures himself defensively that she wouldn't want him to be so alone, that if she were with him now she would approve of his desire for Honoria. But as far as Wales's life is concerned the present is no bastion against his past. For Charlie all time is one time. Events of the past ultimately sour the present and complicate the future.

Not surprisingly, much has been made of Fitzgerald's handling of time in "Babylon Revisited."[11] It is clear that acts of the past haunt the present and threaten defilement of the future. Charlie's memories of Helen evoked in the image of the pendulum movement of her swing do influence his present actions, which will in turn help determine his future with Honoria. The ritual of the daily drink contains both the past and the present and threatens in itself to poison the future. The final irony, however, is not so much that Charlie "sees himself in the eternal present, alone,"[12] but that the past that defeats him is only a *small segment* of his past, that past as defined by Marion and so dreaded by his conscience. That Charlie's proclaimed definition of the past is so different from Marion's indicates both his strength and his weakness. For although Charlie stresses the distant past, a far more extensive time period, in an attempt to refute Marion's emphasis on the much briefer, more immediate past, the considerable merits of the longer time period are relentlessly obscured by the tragic mistakes of the shorter one.

To Marion the past is his year and a half or so of dissipation. She seizes on that one night when Charlie locked Helen out in the snow as a metaphor of his irresponsibility. Fitzgerald seems to be using snow as a part of the central motif of moral laxity, of dissipation, of spiritual bankruptcy. Snow is also a slang term for cocaine and "the Snow Bird" (*Reader* 302) Charlie asks about in the beginning of the opening scene may be a cocaine user or connection.[13] The "snow of twenty-nine" that "wasn't real snow," recalled by Charlie in the final scene, may also refer to the drugs dispensed along with alcohol during those boom days: "If you didn't want it to be snow, you just paid some money" (321). It is especially appropriate that Charlie locks his wife out in "a snowstorm in which she wandered about in slippers" (315). It may be that both snow and cocaine render Helen vulnerable to her fatal "heart trouble" (314), which Marion blames wholly on Charlie. Fitzgerald continually suggests a drug-blurred society in which money was vainly purported to buy not only escape from moral responsibility but immutability from the very laws of nature and from time itself. Placing Charlie's and Helen's marital difficulties in a social scene immersed in both alcohol *and* drugs lends more credence to Marion's condemnations. Although she behaves neurotically during his visits, her importunate brother-in-law's immersion in a destructive lifestyle has given her ample reason to distrust him. On several occasions, Charlie tries to counter Marion's litany of that one terrible night with his own definition of the past. He sees that one night and the year and a half of profligate living as atypical, arguing that he has worked hard for most of his thirty-five years, maintaining that for most of his life he *has been* a responsible person, sober and hardworking.

Charlie Wales (along with hosts of fictional characters under extraordinary pressures, including the protagonists in Dante's *Divine Comedy* and Hemingway's "The Short Happy Life of Francis Macomber") is, at age thirty-five, at the very center of his life, poised between his past and his future, success and failure, heaven and hell. His present claim of reform is more believable because of his long record of past responsibility. The durability of his most recent success in business in Prague is as believable as the likelihood of his overall reform, if one sees as the true norm these many years of sobriety before his relatively brief period of dissipation during the boom years of Paris. The inconsistencies in the numbering of the years before Charlie's stock market success (mistakes which could be either Charlie's or Fitzgerald's) make it difficult to determine some chronological details with certainty. At times the boundary between Charlie's more recent past is as blurred as those scenes that suggest the ambivalence or confusion of values. In any case, Charlie's apparent reform is no more able to prevent Honoria from remaining with the Peterses, away from her father, than Fitzgerald's own self-control was able to overcome Zelda's illness and his own periods of dissipation and prevent him from sending Scottie away from the circle of her true family to the surrogate families of distant boarding schools.

Writing this story around the same time as his brilliant essays "Echoes of the Jazz Age" and "My Lost City," and while Zelda was intermittently institutionalized, Fitzgerald clearly transmutes some of his own guilt feelings, his need for self-justification, his near despair. Concerning this debilitating period he later recorded a haunting summary of his frustrations: how he had "left [his] capacity for hoping on the little roads that led to Zelda's sanitarium."[14] Around the summer (?) of 1930 he imparted to Oscar Forel, Zelda's Swiss psychiatrist, a self-defense whose essence was to be echoed in Charlie Wales's own rationalizations. Fitzgerald wrote: "*During my young manhood for seven years I worked extremely hard*, in six years bringing myself by tireless literary self-discipline to a position of unquestioned preeminence among younger American writers; also by additional 'hack-work' for the cinema, ect. [*sic*]. I gave my wife a comfortable and luxurious life such as few European writers ever achieve."[15]

In a 1979 interview, Scottie Fitzgerald Smith describes how the complexity of the shared guilt between her parents did indeed carry over into the story:

> Question: "Your father said of himself and your mother, Zelda: 'We ruined ourselves. I've never honestly thought we ruined each other.' Does that seem like a basically accurate assessment of their relationship to you?"
>
> Scottie: "Yes. My Aunt Rosalind, my mother's oldest sister, who is portrayed [as Helen's sister] in *Babylon Revisited* [*sic*], was forever trying to prove my father ruined my mother's life. I don't believe that and I don't believe she ruined his life. I think they were singularly mismatched. . . . There's no question but that each needed stability and clearly neither one was able to give the other stability. They encouraged each other's most self-destructive tendencies."[16]

Fitzgerald himself confessed to Scottie (in a letter of June 7, 1940): "I told you once it was an old *Saturday Evening Post* story called 'Babylon Revisited' that I wrote in 1931. You were one of the principal characters." The painful closeness of life and art is even more apparent in Fitzgerald's November 18, 1930, letter to his literary agent Harold Ober, in which he implored: "*Very important* Please *immediately* send me back carbon copy of this story ['Babylon Revisited']. It's terribly important because this is founded on a real quarrel with my sister-in-law + I have to square her."[17] Although he felt his share of the mutual responsibility for the disaster in his own marriage, Fitzgerald may be trying to bury much of the guilt in his fictive counterpart. He works hard to make his alter ego sympathetic. He may also be trying to expiate his own guilt through Charlie's explanations and his rationalizations. Helen's kissing of young Webb is but one indication (perhaps the tip of the iceberg) of her share in the mutual destruction of their marriage and her life.

It is significant that most of Fitzgerald's revisions for the *Taps at Reveille* version of "Babylon Revisited" make Charlie's language more decisive and his character less uncertain. Fitzgerald indicates more precisely in *Taps at Reveille* Charlie's desire to concentrate on the present and change his perspectives. The change from two years since his drinking to three years increases Charlie's separation from his recent past and reinforces his connection with his more distant past as a sober, hardworking husband and father.

But just as Fitzgerald's letter to Dr. Forel contains some of the truth but not the whole truth about the hard work that may not have been sufficient to redeem Fitzgerald's own life, so Charlie Wales's most recent efforts and the stability of his larger past seem not enough to assuage his guilt and repair the damage of the year and a half of shared irresponsibility. And Charlie is up against a fictive force in Helen that is even more formidable than Zelda's Aunt Rosalind, who, according to Scottie, was "forever trying to prove" Fitzgerald had ruined Zelda's life. In the end, Charlie is forced to wait at least six months longer for another chance as Honoria continues to grow out of his fatherly grasp. He must forestall his "desire of putting a little of himself into her before she crystallized utterly" (310). Charlie's fear of Honoria's imminent crystallization may be spawned in part by his memory of that supposedly unreal "snow of twenty-nine" that was, in fact, real enough to threaten the life of another loved one, Helen, his own wife and Honoria's mother. Fitzgerald's letters to Scottie, filled with a poignant urgency, were his attempts from long distance to reach *her* before she "crystallized utterly" without benefit of his stern but loving counsel. For no one believed in strength of character more than Fitzgerald did.

Another important change in the *Taps at Reveille* version of "Babylon Revisited" reinforces the picture of a Charlie struggling toward character reform. Fitzgerald revised the sentence "character, like everything wears out" (*Post* 5) to the more optimistic view of character as an "eternally valuable element" worthy of his trust (*Reader* 306). Some seven years later (July 1938), in a letter to a sixteen-year-old Scottie, Fitzgerald praised "the old virtues of work and courage and the old graces of courtesy and politeness" that came from "my generation of radicals and breakers-down" even though it was a past "that produced Barbara Hutton."[18] We note that Charlie "wanted to jump back a whole generation and trust in character again as the eternally valuable element" (*Reader* 306). Fitzgerald, like Charlie, wanted to be in a position to give Scottie the kind of unassailable love and security that seemed (in 1931) to be epitomized in the home life of Honoria Murphy.

Charlie's desire to repeat his earlier past is charged with the same desperate optimism as Jay Gatsby's attempt to roll back time. Most readers side with Charlie for a variety of reasons. They like him for his optimism, his tenacity of purpose, his hopefulness. They like him for some of the same reasons they like Gatsby. But they also sense his doom. For just as surely as no redemptive phone rings for Gatsby as he lies in the pool of his imminent death, so no testament from the past will save Charlie, who will be forced to forswear, perhaps forever, his hope of regaining Honoria. Nor is Charlie's mask of Charles J. Wales of Prague any more successful in his quest to regain Honoria than was Jimmy Gatz's Gatsby mask in his misguided attempt to regain Daisy. At best he can continue to arrange her life from afar, for, unlike Gatsby, whose own gnawing sense of loss is mercifully foreshortened, Charlie remains alive in the harbor of his hopes. Fitzgerald also tried to remain alive and arrange his daughter's life. Except for brief periodic visits, he too was an absentee breadwinner. Along with Zelda's expensive medical care he gave Scottie's education top priority. At his premature death Scottie's college bills were paid, his legacy of a life insurance policy intact. A kind of model of concern, Charlie also will continue to send Honoria presents, letters, hope. Still, he too seems doomed to "beat on . . . against the current, borne back ceaselessly into the past." And what is as painful to the reader as it is to Charlie is the growing sense that the past gripping him most powerfully is that past so narrowly circumscribed by the prejudiced judgment of Marion. The hope that he can regain legal custody of Honoria is as fleeting as are the highs and lows of his moods that fluctuate throughout the story as a barometer of his complexity.

Yet it is clear as the story ends that the widowed Charlie will continue to provide for his daughter and battle to sustain his own beleaguered sense of honor. For his creator has furnished him an apt model. As a diligent provider for his absentee daughter and institutionalized wife until his poignant death in the prime of his life, Fitzgerald proved himself a superb example of the values he extolled—those old virtues, those old graces, of work and of courage.

NOTES

1. If there is a flaw in "Babylon Revisited" it may be, as my colleague Charles H. Bohner has suggested, in Fitzgerald's fleeting glimpse into Marion's mind (toward the end of section 3) that is inconsistent with the third-person point of view that otherwise remains with Charlie's center of consciousness.

2. Donnelly, *Sara and Gerald*, 148.

3. Fitzgerald, *Reader*, 320. Unless otherwise noted, all subsequent page references to "Babylon Revisited" are to the 1963 edition, are cited as *Reader*, and appear parenthetically in the text.

4. Lanahan, *Scottie*, 45.

5. For a strong case for Charlie's unsuccessful efforts to come to terms with his life, see Toor, "Guilt and Retribution."

6. To the *Taps at Reveille* version of "Babylon Revisited" Fitzgerald added a whole paragraph (his most extensive revision in the story) detailing Charlie's nostalgic tour of Paris (Fitzgerald, *Reader*, 303). It is important to acknowledge that Charlie would, of course, be less than human if his nostalgic memories of those parties of his past were not somewhat sweet as well as bitter, but at this point a rejection of that period of dissipation, even if it be a puritan rejection, is necessary to retain Honoria, the declared purpose of this return visit to Paris.

7. Doc does ultimately give into temptation and drains the bottle. Although Alcoholics Anonymous was not founded until 1935, its firm belief in such total abstinence for alcoholics was established by the 1920s through such organizations as the Oxford Group.

8. For a defense of Wales, in part an answer to Toor, see Twitchell, "'Babylon Revisited': Chronology and Characters."

9. Fitzgerald, "Babylon Revisited," 82; emphasis added. All subsequent page references to the *Saturday Evening Post* version of the story are cited as *Post* and appear parenthetically in the text.

10. Often when Fitzgerald describes physical blurring in many other stories, as well as his novels, he is also implying moral and spiritual uncertainty, weakness, or corruption. It is also clear in, for instance, *The Great Gatsby* and *The Last Tycoon* that attempts to repeat or return to the past are either futile or disastrous.

11. See, for instance, Gross, "Fitzgerald's 'Babylon Revisited'"; and Staley, "Time and Structure." Gross's seminal article remains one of the soundest readings of "Babylon Revisited."

12. Staley, "Time and Structure," 388.

13. For a treatment of Charlie's sense of loss and regret regarding his recent past that also touches upon Fitzgerald's reference to cocaine, see Gervais, "Snow of Twenty-Nine."

14. Fitzgerald, *Notebooks*, 204.

15. Bruccoli and Duggan, *Correspondence of F. Scott Fitzgerald*, 242; emphasis in original.

16. Smith, "Interview," 2–3.

17. Turnbull, *Letters*, 78; Bruccoli, *As Ever*, 175; emphasis in original.

18. Turnbull, *Letters*, 36.

WORKS CITED

Bruccoli, Matthew J., ed., with the assistance of Jennifer McCabe Atkinson. *As Ever, Scott Fitz—: Letters Between F. Scott Fitzgerald and His Literary Agent, Harold Ober—1919–1940*. New York: J. B. Lippincott, 1972.

Bruccoli, Matthew J., and Margaret M. Duggan, eds., with the assistance of Susan Walker. *Correspondence of F. Scott Fitzgerald*. New York: Random House, 1980.

Donnelly, Honoria Murphy. Letter to author, October 16, 1983.

———, with Richard N. Billings. *Sara and Gerald: Villa America and After*. New York: Times Books, 1982.

Fitzgerald, F. Scott. "Babylon Revisited." *Saturday Evening Post*, February 21, 1931, 3–5, 82–84.

———. *The Fitzgerald Reader*. Ed. Arthur Mizener. New York: Scribners, 1963.

———. *The Notebooks of F. Scott Fitzgerald*. Ed. Matthew J. Bruccoli. New York: Harcourt Brace Jovanovich, 1978.

Gervais, Ronald J. "The Snow of Twenty-Nine: 'Babylon Revisited' as *Ubi Sunt* Lament." *College Literature* 7 (1980): 47–52.

Gross, Seymour L. "Fitzgerald's 'Babylon Revisited.'" *College English* 25 (1963): 128–35.

Lanahan, Eleanor. *Scottie the Daughter of . . . : The Life of Frances Scott Fitzgerald Lanahan Smith*. New York: HarperCollins, 1995.

Smith, Scottie Fitzgerald. "An Interview with Scottie Fitzgerald Smith." Philadelphia's *WUHY Press Release*, September 1979: 1–4.

Staley, Thomas F. "Time and Structure in Fitzgerald's 'Babylon Revisited.'" *Modern Fiction Studies* 10 (1964–65): 386–88.

Toor, David. "Guilt and Retribution." *Fitzgerald/Hemingway Annual* 1973: 155–64.

Turnbull, Andrew, ed. *The Letters of F. Scott Fitzgerald*. New York: Scribners, 1963.

Twitchell, James B. "'Babylon Revisited': Chronology and Characters." *Fitzgerald/Hemingway Annual* 1979: 155–360.

VERONICA MAKOWSKY

Noxious Nostalgia: Fitzgerald, Faulkner, and the Legacy of Plantation Fiction

"Why do you hate the South?" asks *Absalom, Absalom!*'s Shreve McCannon, a Canadian, of his Mississippi roommate Quentin Compson. "Panting in the cold air" of Harvard, Quentin "immediately" replies, "I dont hate it . . . *I dont! I dont hate it! I dont hate it!*" (303). For about two hundred years, North Americans, southerners and non-southerners alike, have expressed a similar love–hate fascination with the South, particularly with the mixture of fact and fantasy known as the plantation South. On the one hand there is a nostalgia for a civilization "gone with the wind," a presumably nobler, more gracious, and more cultured life than that of the base, curt, and materialistic modern world. On the other hand there is the plantation as a "platonic conception of the ultimate prison" (Fitzgerald, *Babylon Revisited* 83), where the worst aspects of the national psyche, the materialistic greed that shapes racism and sexism, are perpetually projected and temporarily exorcised. Our great writers not only present the South *both* as American dream and as American nightmare but also are intensely aware of the artist's ambiguous role in creating, perpetuating, and criticizing these myths, as I will later show in Fitzgerald's short story of 1922, "The Diamond as Big as the Ritz," and Faulkner's novel of 1936, *Absalom, Absalom!*[1]

Nostalgia can be defined as a longing for a place, like home, or a time, invariably the past, that cannot be recovered. Nostalgia, then, is intrinsically

From *F. Scott Fitzgerald in the Twenty-first Century*, edited by Jackson R. Bryer, Ruth Prigozy, and Milton R. Stern, pp. 190–201. Copyright © 2003 by the University of Alabama Press.

linked to the pastoral as exemplified in Edenic and Arcadian myths. Critic and historian Lewis P. Simpson argues that "Eden and Arcadia have been symbols of the replacement of the cosmic (the non-conscious or organic) state of human existence with the consciousness of time and history. Simultaneously they have been symbols of an illusory recovery, through pastoral vision and artifice, of the prehistoric state of harmony among God (or gods), man, and nature" (1108). As Simpson suggests, in southern literature the frustrations of nostalgia are exacerbated because nostalgia is manifested as a longing for a state that never existed in the South, that of pastoral innocence. Further, as Simpson notes, "slavery . . . frustrated the desire of the literary mind to project the South as a pastoral homeland" (1109).

For postbellum authors, particularly in the twentieth century, slavery became the fatal temptation that ended the dream of the South as a second Eden, a second chance for mankind. As Walker Percy's protagonist, Dr. Tom More, bitterly muses in *Love in the Ruins* (1971):

> Was it the nigger business from the beginning? What a bad joke: God saying, here it is, the new Eden, and it is yours because you're the apple of my eye; because you the lordly Westerners, the fierce Caucasian-Gentile-Visigoths, believed in me and in the outlandish Jewish event. . . . so I gave it all to you, gave you Israel and Greece and science and art and the lordship of the earth, and finally even gave you the new world that I blessed for you. And all you had to do was pass one little test, which was surely child's play for you because you had already passed the big one. One little test: here's a helpless man in Africa, all you have to do is not violate him. That's all.
>
> One little test: you flunk! (54)

The consequences of that failure are tortuously linked to a hopeless nostalgia for what never was, the plantation as pastoral, in Fitzgerald's "Diamond as Big as the Ritz" and Faulkner's *Absalom, Absalom!*

Before turning to these twentieth-century versions of the plantation myth, though, I would like to present some of the myth's typical features as encapsulated in what is often considered the quintessential plantation nostalgia tale, Thomas Nelson Page's enormously successful "Marse Chan," first published in 1884 and reprinted numerous times.[2] As is characteristic of plantation tales, including those of Fitzgerald and Faulkner, the plot of "Manse Chan" is set in motion by an outsider, like Fitzgerald's John T. Unger or Faulkner's Shreve McCannon, who is in some sense exploring the postbellum South. As Fitzgerald's and Faulkner's narrators will later, Page's narrator stresses the antebellum

South's dreamlike quality as a means of negating the fall into time and history: "Distance was nothing to this people; time was of no consequence to them. . . . [T]he outer world strode by them as they dreamed" (343).

The Edenic atmosphere is enhanced by Page's presentation of a putatively positive South when the outside narrator encounters an elderly former slave called "Uncle Sam" who tells him the tragic tale of the almost incredibly saintly Channing family. As Uncle Sam informs the narrator in the dialect that made these tales so popular with northern audiences, "Dem wuz good ole times, marster" (347). Not only were slaves never whipped on the Channing plantation, but the master blinds himself while saving a slave in a fire. Because of his relatively good situation as a slave, Uncle Sam, as his name suggests, remains patriotic to his cause. That cause is, of course, the Confederacy, but as this tale of reconciliation suggests, this Uncle Sam will turn his allegiance to the national Uncle Sam, despite the nation's racism as demonstrated in Reconstruction politics and in Page's narrator's condescension.

The plantation idyll is what Page and "Marse Chan" are remembered for, but that is an accurate recollection of less than half the story, for Page also shows the evil South in the neighboring Chamberlain plantation. Colonel Chamberlain sells slaves away from their families and feuds with his neighbors over small tracts of land just because his honor is spoiling for a fight. Because he is so preoccupied with pro-secession politics, he neglects his daughter Anne, but then quarrels with her suitor, young Master Channing, over politics and family honor, alienating and dividing the lovers. Anne, a southern belle spoiled by her father and the devotion of young "Marse Chan," clings stubbornly to her family honor and rejects the pleas of her lover until it is too late. Young Master Channing, "Marse Chan" of the title, dies a hero in the war; Anne dies of a broken heart; the Channing and Chamberlain families are extinguished, and so is the Confederacy.

Page, however, is suggesting that the South's fall was not the result of the external machinations of damn Yankees, but rather of its internal failings: the ineffectuality of the southern longing for pastoral of the Channings in the face of crude greed and selfishness, supposedly characteristic of the North, but here embodied in the southern Chamberlains. Page may have felt nostalgia for the pastoral plantation, but he was too fine an artist not to realize that it never existed and to acknowledge the actual South's affinity with national values. Indeed, that affinity to American values may have contributed greatly to the tremendous popularity of "Marse Chan," in that the racism and materialism manifested in the tale were not foreign to the North but could be safely projected onto the supposedly "exotic" South and punished there as part of the Reconstruction drama of penance and purgation that led to the ultimate in nostalgia, the Lost Cause, celebrated by both North and South.

F. Scott Fitzgerald had great admiration for Page's work; in fact, in 1922, the same year in which he published "The Diamond as Big as the Ritz," he suggested to Maxwell Perkins that Scribner's republish Page's *In Ole Virginia*, which includes "Marse Chan," as one of eighteen titles that Fitzgerald was proposing for a reprint series (Bruccoli, *Some Sort of Epic Grandeur* 153–54). Faulkner, of course, was highly familiar with the plantation tradition, and his borrowings from and reworkings of other stories from *In Ole Virginia* indicate his familiarity with that collection, a topic too large to be addressed here. Fitzgerald's "The Diamond as Big as the Ritz" and Faulkner's *Absalom, Absalom!* share significant similarities with and differences from Page's "Marse Chan" and other plantation tales, manifesting their need to participate in and revise the great American cultural melodrama of the fall from the second Eden into a time and history of pain and labor.

Like Page, Fitzgerald and Faulkner depict the fall of the plantation world as a result of inhumane values—not Yankeedom as deus ex machina, but Yankee materialism carried to its logical and horrific extreme.[3] Fitzgerald's Braddock Washington, significantly named for the father of the whole country who was first a southerner, owns a Montana plantation, suggesting the spread of materialism to the western United States. The plantation is complete with slaves and set atop a "diamond as big as the Ritz." The family leads a life of luxurious pastoral bliss based on a cold, hard rock whose worth is man-made; a diamond won't feed or clothe anyone, making the parody of the southern cotton plantation even more extreme. Echoing southern xenophobic defensiveness at Yankee incursions, Mr. Washington thinks nothing of murdering anyone who strays onto his plantation for fear they would betray the secret of his "peculiar institution" for producing wealth. Ironically, he is in effect a land-poor southern aristocrat, for if he tried to sell any of his diamond, the flooded markets would crash from the oversupply, making his treasure trash. In pro-slavery tracts, southern plantation owners would bemoan the fact that they were the real slaves, chained to their patriarchal white man's burden of taking care of the slaves and their acreage. Fitzgerald satirizes this plaint by showing Braddock Washington as enslaved to his materialism, unable to leave his huge, cold rock, bound by his own territorial greed.

In *Absalom, Absalom!* Faulkner similarly depicts the causes of the southern fall from the second Eden as internal yet external, the result of the internalization of American racism and materialism as embodied in southern slavery. Mr. Compson tells his son Quentin about Mr. Coldfield, who starved to death in his attic rather than support the Confederacy and so "would not be present on the day when the South would realize that it was now paying the price for having erected its economic edifice not on the rock of stern morality but on the shifting sands of moral opportunism and brigandage" (209). While

Mr. Coldfield is as sanctimonious and ineffectual as Page's Channings, he does recognize the falsity of the southern pastoral ideal. The central character of the novel, Thomas Sutpen, like Braddock Washington, is enslaved by his obsession with maintaining his acreage. Indeed, the name of his plantation, Sutpen's Hundred, suggests that Sutpen has become the plantation, part of a system that can be counted and valued. Immediately after the war, Sutpen frantically and futilely tries to keep every one of his hundred acres from the clutches of carpetbagger tax collectors, but in his monomania he loses most of his family and, ultimately, his life.

Unlike Page, however, Fitzgerald and Faulkner have a much more openly ambiguous view of the ultimate materialism, slavery. From one perspective, their fictive slaves are like Page's eternally devoted Uncle Sam. Sutpen's "wild niggers" work desperately beside their master in his attempt to found his plantation, making no attempt to escape. In Clytie, his daughter by one of the slave women, Sutpen manages to make a slave in his own, if darker, image, and she remains on the Sutpen plantation throughout all of its vicissitudes until she burns to death in defense of Sutpen's son Henry at the end of the novel. The slaves of Fitzgerald's Braddock Washington are even more stereotypically faithful. Like a mammy, the seemingly emasculated Gygsum, the slave designated as body servant to John T. Unger, undresses, bathes, and dresses him. When Washington tells his slaves that Confederate general Nathan B. Forrest, a notorious antebellum slave trader, "had reorganized the shattered southern armies and defeated the North in one pitched battle, . . . they passed a vote declaring it a good thing and held revival services immediately" (87–88). Fitzgerald makes us well aware that they are mindlessly demonstrating their faith in the institutions that have helped brainwash them: a democracy in which they cannot participate and a Christianity that is perverted to stress their obedience, not their worth as souls.

Yet Fitzgerald and Faulkner emphasize one curious detail about the Washington and Sutpen slaves that calls the image of the "happy darky" into question. Sutpen's slaves, who actually speak a version of Caribbean French, a Creole, are suspected by Mississippians of speaking "some dark and fatal tongue of their own" (27). Braddock Washington's slaves have "lived so long apart from the world that their original dialect has become an almost indistinguishable patois" (93). The master class thus tells itself that the slaves are subhuman, as manifested in their incomprehensible sounds, but Faulkner and Fitzgerald are pointing to a justifiable paranoia of slave owners, terrified of slave revolts hatched with secrecy and codes; the slaves, after all, have honed their survival skill of telling the masters only what they want to hear, reinforcing the myth of the plantation pastoral peopled by "happy darkies." Fitzgerald and Faulkner are satirically suggesting that the masters have made themselves subhuman, in that they cannot recognize the slaves as human, cannot speak the same language, and cannot tell truth from falsehood.

Like the slaves and like Page's Anne Chamberlain, Fitzgerald's and Faulkner's women characters are damaged by their allegiance to the ideology that thwarts their human potential. Braddock Washington's youngest daughter, Kismine, is the perfect southern belle.[4] She is the embodiment of the plantation's Edenic ideal: "Just think," she tells John T. Unger, "I'm absolutely fresh ground." Like the marble statues on pedestals to which southern women were often compared, atop her mountain Kismine is "the incarnation of physical perfection" (90) and pure. As she tells John, "I'm very innocent and girlish. I never smoke, or drink, or read anything except poetry. I know scarcely any mathematics or chemistry. I dress *very* simply—in fact, I scarcely dress at all" (91). Fitzgerald, though, is suggesting that such Edenic near-nudity is artificial, since it is maintained at a tremendous cost of isolation for the belle and the exploitation of others. Kismine's very self-conscious tally of her purity suggests how contrived it really is.

Similarly, Faulkner's women in *Absalom, Absalom!* embody the plantation ideal and lose their humanity. Sutpen's second wife, Ellen Coldfield, comes from family that is respectable, though not rich or aristocratic. When she marries Sutpen, she takes up bellehood with a vengeance, shopping and chattering in a fantasy world that she believed could not end. Like Kismine's need to point out her purity, Ellen's need to work so hard at bellehood also points out its artificial quality in an already-declining and soon-to-be fallen world. When the harsh reality of the Civil War intrudes, Ellen fades and dies rather than confront it. As Mr. Compson tells Quentin, "Apparently Ellen had now served her purpose, completed the bright afternoon of the butterfly's summer and vanished" (61). From her training in southern ideology, Ellen is incapable of saving herself or her children, including her daughter Judith, who will die an impoverished spinster, still loyal to her father's progeny and to his "design." Had Judith rebelled against her father and eloped with Charles Bon, despite the possibilities of incest and miscegenation, much of the tragedy could have been avoided; but like Page's Anne and Fitzgerald's Kismine, Judith is unable to think beyond the law of the fathers. Also like them, she is too loyal to the pastoral ideal to see the menacing reality.

The way the pastoral ideal of the plantation demands a remoteness from real human concerns is suggested by the many references to dreams in *Absalom, Absalom!* and "The Diamond as Big as the Ritz." To some extent, this is reminiscent of Page's dreamlike Virginia, but as in the case of the supposedly "happy darkies" and belles, Fitzgerald and Faulkner add a sinister emphasis. Of Thomas Sutpen's impossible desire to reestablish Sutpen's Hundred after the war, Miss Rosa Coldfield says that "if he was mad, it was only his compelling dream that was insane, not his methods" (134); there was method, but it was madness because his dream consisted of an exclusive dynasty ruling in perpetuity over acres and human beings. Of John T. Unger's temporary seduction into Braddock Washington's dream world, Fitzgerald writes, "Everybody's youth is a dream, a form of chemical madness" (113). The fantasy of the plantation myth is immature, a form of addictive madness when held into maturity by grown men like Washington and Sutpen.

In contrast to the nostalgic tone of Page's story, Fitzgerald's and Faulkner's tales also show that the greatest immaturity, the deepest madness, is the Gatsby-like nostalgia for repeating the past, a past that was never as ideal as the prospective revenant believes. After the war, Thomas Sutpen acts as if "there might not have been any war at all, or it was on another planet" (130) when, at age fifty-nine, he self-destructively attempts a young man's herculean effort of rebuilding an antebellum plantation under Reconstruction conditions. Similarly, after the destruction of the Montana plantation is commenced by men in recently invented "aeroplanes," Braddock Washington desperately tries to bribe God with the world's grandest shrine if "matters should be as they were yesterday at this hour and that they should so remain" (109). The irony of nostalgia is that if the past could be repeated, the consequences would be the same unhappy ones, yet that is what nostalgia so strongly denies.

The isolation of the plantation, also remarked by Page, helps to maintain the owner's pathological immaturity and fixation on the past, according to Faulkner and Fitzgerald. As Thomas Sutpen obsessively worked to establish his plantation before the war, he immured himself at Sutpen's Hundred. When he decided that he needed other people in order to found his dynasty, the townsfolk of Jefferson were so alienated that they refused to attend his wedding and threw trash and garbage as the wedding party emerged from the church. After the war, when Sutpen is asked by local landowners to join the Klan in an attempt to repel carpetbaggers and scalawags, he replies that "if every man in the South would do as he himself was doing, would see to the restoration of his own land, the general land of the South would save itself" (130). While his refusal to join the Klan may seem praiseworthy, his isolationist reasoning is not, for Sutpen is advocating that southern society be remade in the image of its most perfect exemplar, himself. Braddock Washington also wants to believe that he can remove himself from the larger world, going so far as to murder visitors so that they cannot lead more outsiders into his paradise of narcissism. He, like Sutpen, is a tyrant, not the pastoral plantation's avatar of southern hospitality, and so he refuses guests, telling his son, "This is where the United States ends" (80).

Faulkner and Fitzgerald, of course, do not believe that the United States ends at the plantation's boundaries, since Sutpen's and Washington's destroyed plantations can also be prophetic of "where the United States" could "end" since nation and plantation share some of the same values. Sutpen has a "design" that he will found a plantation where a poor white boy would not be turned away at the front door as he had been as a poor white boy in his youth (210). His aims of refuge and inclusion recall those of the founders of another plantation, Plymouth Plantation, who were also looking for a chance to redeem history and reclaim purity (Puritans) by founding a "city upon a hill" as an example to those still mired in history. However, as Sutpen's plantation was a refuge only for whites, not blacks, Plymouth Plantation was a refuge only for white Puritans, not other religious sects or other races such as Native Americans; intolerance and ethnocentricity doom the new Eden. Thomas Sutpen does turn a young man away: he rejects his firstborn son, Charles Bon, when he learns that his wife has some "black blood." Charles is killed by his half brother, Sutpen's son Henry, because of the threat of incest and miscegenation in the proposed marriage between Charles and Henry's sister Judith, and Henry himself flees into decades of exile. Because of his inability to accept his first son's racial heritage, Sutpen destroys both sons and his design of a pastoral plantation. Because of the racism that he shares with the plantation South and the antebellum North, his design ends not in a pastoral idyll but in the howls of his black and mentally deficient descendant near the ruins of the Plantation house. In one of his characteristic inversions, Faulkner does not suggest "If you can't beat 'em, join 'em," but rather "If you won't let 'em join you, they will beat you."

Braddock Washington shares a similar pastoral vision that thinly masks a lack of true southern hospitality. With devastating irony from Fitzgerald, Washington, like Sutpen, observes that "his one care must be the protection of his secret lest in the possible panic attendant on its discovery he should be reduced with all the property-owners of the world to utter poverty" (89). His secret, like Sutpen's design, appears to be the plantation as Eden, or America's "fresh, green breast of the new world." As it does for Sutpen, it ends for Washington who is, after all, a descendant of the slaveholding Father of Our Country, "among the ruins of a vista that had been a garden spot that morning" (106). The southern Arcadia, the American dream, transforms itself into nightmare because "the United States ends here" unless you belong to the small, exclusive, dominant group.

What, then, is the artist's place in this pastoral dream become nightmare? Page's "Marse Chan" suggests that the artist's role is to preserve, celebrate, and mourn the beneficent aspects of the plantation dream, despite the subliminal doubts that Page expressed through the noble plantation owners' malevolent doubles. "Marse Chan" contains no artists or artist figures who question this cultural imperative, unlike "The Diamond as Big as the Ritz"

or *Absalom, Absalom!* For Fitzgerald and Faulkner, such artists do not participate willingly, like Page, but are abducted into cultural servitude. Braddock
Washington "had caused to be kidnapped a landscape gardener, an architect,
a designer of stage settings, and a French decadent poet left over from the last
century. . . . But one by one they had shown their uselessness. . . . [T]hey all
went mad . . . and were now confined comfortably in an insane asylum" (98).
Washington's chateau is completed by what Fitzgerald and Faulkner regarded
as meretricious, but what they both attempted unsuccessfully to become, "a
moving-picture fella" (*Babylon Revisited* 98). The true artists are driven to
insanity by unappreciative patrons and audiences who may not want to hear
the truth about the plantation and much prefer the comforting fantasies of
Hollywood's *Gone with the Wind*.[5]

Thomas Sutpen wants a plantation house that sounds remarkably similar to the one Braddock Washington actually built. Sutpen imports a French
architect to design it, but as Faulkner's narrator comments, "only an artist
could have borne Sutpen's ruthlessness and hurry and still manage to curb the
dream of grim and castlelike magnificence at which Sutpen obviously aimed"
(29). Despite his success in checking Sutpen's vulgar display, the architect is
also effectively kidnapped, since when he attempts to leave Sutpen's Hundred
he is hunted like an animal by Sutpen and his "wild niggers." When captured,
he "flung" his "hand up in a gesture that [Quentin's] grandfather said you
simply could not describe, that seemed to gather all misfortune and defeat
that the human race ever suffered into a pinch in his fingers like dust and
flung it backward over his head" (207). Although Sutpen's architect does not
go mad like Washington's artists, his gesture of resignation and abdication
indicates that he too is institutionalized into the particular madness, the "misfortune and defeat," of plantation culture, and of the American culture that
likes to buy into that nostalgic myth in the form of fiction and films; yet like
Fitzgerald and Faulkner, the architect does not surrender and keeps pursuing
art within his captivity.

Perhaps the most chilling aspect of Fitzgerald's and Faulkner's cri-
tiques of nostalgia is their depiction of nostalgia's effect on the future as
represented by John T. Unger and Quentin Compson, who are too pos-
sessed by nostalgia's chimeras to move into the future. For John, all that
lingers is the "shabby gift of disillusion" (113). Quentin tells Shreve, "I am
older at twenty than a lot of people who have died" (301). While the nostalgia that is so characteristic of plantation fiction might appear to be a
harmless if somewhat sentimental indulgence in fantasy, the portraits of
John and Quentin indicate that their creators think otherwise. In "The Diamond as Big as the Ritz" and *Absalom, Absalom!* they show how great fiction
can convert seductive fantasies about the past into compelling truths about

the consequences of belittling and misrepresenting the past. For Fitzgerald and Faulkner, the nostalgia of the plantation myth misrepresents the past, devalues the present, and strangles the future.

Notes

1. In its evocation of an agrarian and uncomplicated idyll in an increasingly urbanized and industrialized America, the plantation myth has been particularly popular with the non-southern audiences who enthusiastically consumed it, from antebellum John Pendleton Kennedy's *Swallow Barn* (1832) through Thomas Nelson Page's postbellum nostalgia tales, and into the twentieth century with Margaret Mitchell's *Gone with the Wind* (1936). For an overview of the genre in Page's era, see MacKethan. For an overview in the twentieth century, see Bargainnier.

2. Like Fitzgerald, Page has been considered a victim of his own early success whose late works were too serious and socially conscious for the expectations of his audience, yet whose artistry can be seen throughout his career, with or without the trappings of the plantation myth; see Cash; Flusche; Theodore Gross; Holman; Simms; and Wilson, *Patriotic Gore*.

3. Critics such as Brooks, Rodewald, Scholes, and Sklar have compared Thomas Sutpen with Jay Gatsby, but they have not explored the comparison with Braddock Washington.

4. Donaldson, "Scott Fitzgerald's Romance," examines Fitzgerald's explicitly southern belles and the history of his fascination with the South.

5. Roulston, "Whistling 'Dixie' in Encino," parallels the southern plantation with the world of the Hollywood studio in *The Last Tycoon*. Way compares Washington's chateau to a Hollywood set (69).

RONALD BERMAN

Fitzgerald and the Geography of Progress

We see the connected and opposed regions of North and South in many of Fitzgerald's stories and novels: "The Ice Palace" (May 1920), "The Jelly-Bean" (October 1920), "Two For a Cent" (April 1922), "The Diamond as Big as the Ritz" (June 1922), *The Beautiful and Damned* (1922), "Dice, Brassknuckles & Guitar" (May 1923), "The Third Casket" (May 1924), "The Sensible Thing" (July 1924), *The Great Gatsby* (1925), "The Dance" (June 1926), "The Last of the Belles" (March 1929), "Basil and Cleopatra" (April 1929), "Two Wrongs" (January 1930), "Flight And Pursuit" (May 1932), "Family in the Wind" (June 1932).[1] Simply by recalling the tenor of these works we can begin to understand their thematic importance. There is, clearly, a *modern* conflict between North and South.[2] The War between the States takes on contemporary shape in these works. The new war involves our national character and purpose. It sets certain traditional values against those of progress and success. We are intended to rethink—as Fitzgerald himself did—not only our Victorian past but historical time itself.

There were a number of American Dreams in the twenties, and Robert Nisbet reminds us that some of them had a theology: "Faith in mankind's advance to an even better future assumed the same kind of evangelical zeal, especially among the American masses, that is associated with religion."[3] That seems to be accurate—we recall that *The Rise of American Civilization*

From *Modernity and Progress: Fitzgerald, Hemingway, Orwell*, pp. 13–23, 101–04. Copyright © 2005 by the University of Alabama Press.

had in 1927 connected our "invulnerable faith" in the means of technology to the end of "unlimited progress."[4] Nisbet, like Charles A. and Mary R. Beard, reminds us that our native, material version of the Idea of Progress was not killed off by the Great War. In fact, it was "never more compelling than during the first four or five decades of the twentieth century."[5] Not everyone agreed with this variant of civic religion. Yet, despite the satire of writers like H. L. Mencken and Sinclair Lewis, it was indeed conventional to think that prosperity incarnated the Idea of Progress.

F. Scott Fitzgerald was among those who took the notion with a grain of salt. We think almost automatically of Gatsby presiding over his transformation, looking first at the windows of his palace and then at every one of his doors and towers and counting the years it took to buy them. But property offers the same problem to literature as to philosophy. Towns, buildings, and markets are ephemeral. They inevitably become reminders of material limits. The same images used by advertisers to celebrate growth were used by writers of the twenties to reverse the common judgment about it. Van Wyck Brooks wrote about pioneer cities no longer populated, ghost towns "all but obliterated in alkali dust." Fitzgerald wrote about the entropic ruins of the American landscape in the village of Fish and the Valley of Ashes.[6] He often used architectonic images—arrogant towers, faded mansions, bungalow tracts crawling along farm fields, even one particular broken-down billboard—to suggest defeated *national* expectations. These things were, after all, imagery in the public realm.[7]

There is in Fitzgerald not only an idea of but a geography of progress. When Nick Carraway organizes Gatsby's funeral, he asks Mr. Gatz if he "might want to take the body west." But the answer is that "Jimmy always liked it better down East."[8] Both remarks need their context. Fitzgerald's description of America rests on a real and also metaphorical sense of geography. As to the first, his map consists of familiar quadrants: North, South, East, and West. As to the second, East and North, conventionally the same, are poised against West—and especially against South. The East opposes other regions and is understood in relation to them. That should be factored into our understanding of passages that seem confined to geographical meanings. Here, for example, is Tom Buchanan on New York:

> "Oh, I'll stay in the East, don't you worry," he said, glancing at Daisy and then back at me as if he were alert for something more. "I'd be a God Damn fool to live anywhere else." (12)

On the face of it this is unmysterious, conveying information the same way Mr. Gatz does when he tells Nick that Jimmy "rose up to his position in the East" (131). But Tom both asserts and conceals. He is from monied Chicago—and H. L. Mencken had just written that rich men come from "the fat lands of the Middle West" to New York because "the ordinary American law does not run there."[9] Mencken is not referring solely to the Volstead Act; his essay is about sexual opportunism in commercial form. In Mencken, Metropolis is a marketplace of commodities, including things human. "There is little in New York," he writes in another essay of 1927, "that does not spring from money."[10] It is reasonably plain in *The Great Gatsby* that Tom's affair with Myrtle is a transaction. Myrtle knows a lot about price and marketplace values. She despises her husband for having borrowed a suit for their wedding, falls in love, in part, with Tom's own shoes and suit and high style, uses his money to transform her own social class from blue-collar to bourgeois. Myrtle knows about two subjects important to Mencken and to his theme: everything is for sale, and "most of these fellas will cheat you every time" (27). Cheating is the essential mode of capitalism in Mencken's New York essays. He provides a long catalog of terms like "exploiter," "merchants," "customer," "sharper," and "bawds and pimps," which define each other while defining the economy. Notably, he writes about bootlegging as the central "industry" of Metropolis.[11] The East, the home of progress, embodies serious contradictions.

Fitzgerald wrote that his story "May Day" shows his attempt to "weave . . . into a pattern" his experience of living in New York.[12] The meaning of that pattern is displayed in the story's opening—and is reinforced by ideas in circulation at the time. New York is the incarnation of marketplace values that are "hymned by the scribes and poets" of advertising (98). We know that writers resisted the confusion of progress with prosperity. They were not satisfied by industrial democracy and resented its commercialism. More than anything, they resented its claims. Toward the end of the decade, in *A Preface to Morals*, Walter Lippmann stated that the theory of "mechanical progress" was the latest false religion.[13] Lewis Mumford located this inflation of values in New York, which was the East incarnate: "Broadway, in sum, is the façade of the American city: a false front. The highest achievements of our material civilization—and at their best our hotels, our department stores, and our Woolworth towers are achievements—count as so many symptoms of its spiritual failure. In order to cover up the vacancy of getting and spending in our cities, we have invented a thousand fresh devices for getting and spending. As a consequence our life is externalized."[14]

Fitzgerald's writings of the early twenties invoke "devices for getting and spending" in the form of advertised commodities.[15] Artifacts appear everywhere in the fiction, like these from "The Last of the Belles": "I stumbled here and there in the knee-deep underbrush, looking for my youth in a clapboard

or a strip of roofing or a rusty tomato can" (462). Roland Marchand's *Advertising the American Dream* remarks of copy text and image that such objects
had already entered the nation's visual vocabulary in the twenties. To refer
to them is to refer to the vast and necessarily false metonym of progress.
When that tomato can had first been described, it was in the language of
superlatives and even adulation; it meant future satisfaction and not only in a
material way.[16] Fitzgerald's extraordinary images of decay in the public realm
constitute a formidable argument against progress. Marchand identifies the
imagery of the *new* with a social apologetic:

> Civilization ... had found a way to regain Nature's intended
> gifts without sacrificing the fruits of progress.... In proclaiming
> the victories over threats to health and beauty that the products
> of civilization now made possible, these parables of Civilization
> Redeemed never sought to denigrate Nature.... Civilization,
> which had brought down the curse of Nature upon itself, had still
> proved capable of discovering products that would enable Nature's
> original and beneficent intentions to triumph.... the advance of
> civilization ... need never exact any real losses. Civilization had
> become its own redeemer.[17]

Fitzgerald has his own notion of civilization, expressed by contravening
images. In "The Ice Palace" we see colors "of light gold and dark gold and shiny
red" dominating the Bellamy library. These are the colors of money and desire.
But the books appear to be unread—they are objects and artifacts, as in the later
scene of Jay Gatsby's own library. The more important point is the opposition
of cost and value in the Bellamy household, a place specifically identified with
cost and value in the North. Unmediated wealth has accumulated only "a lot
of fairly expensive things ... that all looked about fifteen years old" (56). These
commodities have no past—which makes them perfect objective correlatives
for wealth without history, that is, for progress without meaning.

Because the North is where progress happens, it is bound to display
the uneasy connection between prosperity and progress. Fitzgerald disputes
that connection repeatedly. In his fiction, "success" involuntarily aspires to a
higher, moralized form of itself. Even the provincial Mr. Gatz believes that
his son would have "helped build up the country" (131) if he had lived. Our
civic religion holds that the accumulated sum of individual successes adds
up to national progress. This was the promise of the North. But, even in the
South, our duty is to change and improve.

Fitzgerald's stories about the South point out the failure of unaided
"tradition." The mention of that phrase in the twenties assumes the need to

recall and even to embody the past. Yet, in Fitzgerald's South, evolution is imperative: the Jelly-bean realizes that he has to "make somethin'" out of his farm and his life (157); Sally Carrol Happer explains that she needs "to live where things happen" (51). Sara Haardt, who grew up in Montgomery with Zelda Sayre, understood the necessity for change—or at least of escape: "Oh, no use talking, the South was sweet. But it was a sweetness tinged with the melancholy of death. It was because beauty, somehow, is shorter lived in the South than in the North, or in the West; and beauty, more than mere survival, is the most poignant proof of life."[18] In "The Ice Palace" Fitzgerald dealt with this conception through the idea of the *vita activa*. Evanescence was the field of vitality.

"Dice, Brassknuckles & Guitar" is a regional parable of the early twenties. Its central figure, Jim Powell, is southern, romantic, chivalrous, unsophisticated. He sees things with great clarity but no perspective. Jim is on his way north to the land of money and opportunity. Equipped with the kinds of knowledge implied by the story's title, he is innocent of the knowledge of how the social world works. By the end of the story he offends his wealthy patrons, is put in his place, and then is forced to leave. Present works against past in this story, as city works against province. Fitzgerald's language dwells insistently on "Victorian" qualities of character, mind, and landscape. He was of two minds about the meaning of that phrase. It could mean what Wells, Shaw, and Strachey intended it to mean, serving as a synonym for outmoded ideas. But it also meant a connection to time, place, and even to one's own beginnings: "here and there lie patches of garden country dotted with old-fashioned frame mansions, which have wide shady porches and a red swing on the lawn. And perhaps, on the widest and shadiest of the porches there is even a hammock left over from the hammock days, stirring gently in a mid-Victorian wind." The passing tourist "can't see the hammock from the road—but sometimes there's a girl in the hammock" (237). In this story the term "Victorian" does not suggest repressiveness. The opposite is suggested, as if the past had something to offer at least as important as "the twentieth century" did. There is in fact a girl in the hammock; her name, Amanthis, connotes (according to the *Oxford English Dictionary*) both love and belief. The text argues through images. It tells us not only that she has wonderful yellow hair but that "there was something enormously yellow about the whole scene" (238). The language offers a prevision of the yellow and gold in *The Great Gatsby*, colors that symbolize promise. But the Victorian scene cannot contain those feelings generated within it. Amanthis is attracted to Jim Powell, who brings to the monied North a sense of style and idea long since forgotten. But he is disarmed by his innocence, and she by her sophistication. He will return to the ever more eccentric South; she will become part of the ever more progressive North. A sleeping beauty quite literally awakens in this story, but Harold Lloyd is in a role that needs Tyrone Power.

In "The Ice Palace" Sally Carrol Happer has her own "awakening." Both stories begin with real and figurative possibilities. In Fitzgerald, the idea of "beginning" often needs to be qualified because an opening may be a continuation of history: "The sunlight dripped over the house like golden paint over an art jar, and the freckling shadows here and there only intensified the rigor of the bath of light. Up in her bedroom window Sally Carrol Happer rested her nineteen-year-old chin on a fifty-two-year old sill" (48). It seems unlikely that "Life in Tarleton, Georgia, after all, nurtured only the most negative aspects of romantic egotism." Nor do I think that such passages are meant to be viewed under the aspect of Tennyson's "Lotos-Eaters."[19] The argument that the South was an example of cultural enervation was commonplace enough before Fitzgerald's story appeared, but it took a different slant. The region was agrarian in an industrial age and fundamentalist in an age of skepticism. As seen by H. L. Mencken the South had no textual culture: its poets, historians, and novelists were simply a national joke. But Fitzgerald was not much concerned with Baptist morality or with literary amateurism.[20] To worry about those things was to confuse ideas with essences.

Fitzgerald's southern characters are important because their minds and manners have been shaped by time and place. In the first part of "The Ice Palace" time is more than referential; it is a protagonist. Sally Carrol Rapper keeps returning to the graveyard in Tarleton because it is history objectified. Like Fitzgerald himself, she is of two minds about past and present. She knows how important it is to use her energies, to operate within the realm of material substance. She is not an innocent and knows that money and power are the means of life. But she also values the style of life that understands money and power to be means and not ends. She is an idealist, and Santayana had observed in 1920 that American idealism is material to the extent that it "goes hand in hand with present contentment and with foresight of what the future very likely will actually bring."[21] That idealism wants to work, achieve, produce. As Sally Carrol puts the issue, the "sort of energy" she has "may be useful somewhere" (51). Energy needs a field of action, and the North provides that. But without the past, Santayana writes, Americans could have no "fixity in human morals, in institutions, or in ideas." Necessarily (and we think of Fitzgerald's invocations of "Victorian" permanence and southern stasis), "America is full of mitigations of Americanism. There are survivals; there are revolts; there is a certain hesitation in the main current itself, carrying the nation towards actions and sentiments not altogether congruous with experimental progress."[22] His conclusion applies to Sally Carrol Happer and also to Charlie Wales in "Babylon Revisited," who "wanted to jump back a whole generation" (619). As Stanley Brodwin put it, certain of Fitzgerald's stories show "the tension between living presence and its gift of ontological triumph through a past, lost moment of history on the one hand and ongoing personal experience on the other."[23]

The South is more than "a warm, pleasant, and lazy place, a home of good manners and elegant traditions, a garden which, for Fitzgerald, grew Southern belles and jelly-beans."[24] The South must mean more than that if only because *it exists in relation to the North*. In making a point about dominant national values, Milton R. Stern observes that the worship of industriousness had been corrupted: "ideologies of work, responsibility, politeness, respect, decency, had been perverted and bastardized" in the pursuit of wealth. These, I think, are northern virtues, and they have remade the nation. If they prove false, then there is not much leverage for criticism of the South because the connection between regions is dialectical.

Stern's comment on Fitzgerald—that he "chooses community and history"[25]—is worth recalling. Such choice was difficult: in 1922, Harold E. Stearns began *Civilization in the United States* with the argument that "We have no heritages or traditions to which to cling except those that have already withered in our hands and turned to dust."[26] That, essentially, is the problem posed by Fitzgerald's stories about the conflictual relationship of North and South, or of progress and tradition. It may be that *both* progress and tradition are fictions. Cleanth Brooks writes that there are really two myths of American history. One of these is the idea of the Old South, rooted gracefully in time. The other is the idea of the New North, advancing into the future: "If there is a myth of the Southern past, we must recognize that there is a myth of the American future—its more respectable name is the American Dream—and with reference to the charge that the Southern myth erred in describing its past as golden, one might point out that the American myth has consistently insisted that its future was made of the same precious metal."[27] Fitzgerald seems to have understood that one myth of American life might be no more convincing than the other. He was not engaged by the northern ideology, which he knew differed greatly from its material forms. In 1923, he stated that Chicago and St. Paul had "wealth without background, tradition, or manners."[28] Just before this, in 1922, he had described the Southern "tradition of before-the-war culture" with this summary phrase: "most of which is false."[29]

Two of Fitzgerald's stories of the early twenties suggest southern "community and history" in terms of opposed ideas. The first of these stories, "Two For A Cent," refers itself to those golden colors of *The Great Gatsby* and of the primeval South: A yellow sky is seen by a man sitting on "an immemorial bench, for the sky was every shade of yellow, the color of tan, the color of gold, the color of peaches." The view of red buildings and yellow sky "was beautiful" and like a "dream."[30] Fitzgerald customarily thinks in colors, and we know that these colors mattered to him. But against the new-world colors of the horizon are human facts. Fitzgerald, who takes the idea of community literally, may have more to say about houses than Jane Austen. In the new South, "Bungalows . . . were reproducing their species . . . as though by some monstrous affiliation with the guinea-pig; it was the most common type of house in the country. It was a house built by a race whose more energetic complement hoped either to move up or move on" (34). The last line identi-fies the northern style of energy and progress without direction as it has come unbidden to Fitzgerald's "Immemorial" South.

In at least one case, Fitzgerald arrived at a compromise. Fittingly enough, it is stated in a form bordering on fantasy. His story "The Third Casket" fol-lows (at a distance) act 1 of *The Merchant of Venice*. In Shakespeare, Portia is advised that "Your father was ever virtuous, and holy men at their death have good inspirations; therefore the lottery that he hath devised in these three chests of gold, silver, and lead, whereof who chooses his meaning chooses you, will no doubt never be chosen by any rightly but one who you shall rightly love."[31] Fitzgerald paid a good deal of attention to this passage but even more to a certain interpretation of its meaning.

"The Third Casket" has something to do with the inheriting daughter, Lola, but is in fact about her father, Cyrus Girard, a worried Wall Street broker of sixty who seems singularly free of any good inspirations. He offers his business and his daughter to the one of three men who does the best job of making money. The story rests—uncomfortably—on myth and fantasy: as Girard puts it, the winner will get what fairy tales give, "half my king-dom and, if she wants him, my daughter's hand" (88). So far, the story is an approximation of Portia's story and of those tales located on the unseen edges of *The Great Gatsby*. But dividing up a kingdom ought to give us a different kind of clue. This is not wholly about *The Merchant of Venice* nor wholly about Shakespeare.

Fitzgerald's title comes from Freud's recent essay "The Theme of the Three Caskets," which had memorably been applied to *King Lear*.[32] In *King Lear* and in Fitzgerald's story we see an old man perilously close to dying unregenerate. And, as Freud states of that tragedy, "the relationship of a father to his children, which might be a fruitful source of many dramatic situations, is not turned to further account."[33] Nor is it here. Fitzgerald's Portia has only a minor role; the old man is on center stage. His fate is the issue. Nothing in *The Merchant of Venice* corresponds to Fitzgerald's plot, which begins with an old man saying that Americans don't know what to do with their lives. The middle of the story is about middle age, the end about the coming of death. These are in fact the death themes of Freud's essay. He saw in the scene of choosing three daughters or "caskets" a way of understanding the ordinary conditions of life: "A choice is made where in reality there is obedience to a compulsion." That is to say, in choosing what is most humble, and what most resembles a leaden coffin, death is "recognized intellectually."[34] The father comes to terms with reality in Freud and also in Fitzgerald. His story is their plot.

There are other themes common to Freud and to Fitzgerald. According to the former, "King Lear's dramatic story" shows "that one should not give up one's possessions and rights during one's lifetime."[35] But I think the main connection resides in Cyrus Girard's awareness that "fairy tales" may after all correspond to life. Freud's essay refers particularly to Cinderella, the stories of Paris and of Psyche, and "The Twelve Brothers" and "The Six Swans" of the Brothers Grimm. They are all fables of loss and regeneration, important for Freud's argument of symbolic representation.

Fitzgerald's own fable in the stories I have listed was the mystical marriage of North and South. It was clearly one way of looking at his divided American allegiances, at his own marriage, and at the romantic tensions of his novels and stories. There are too many North–South oppositions to disregard. In certain of his stories, a marriage fails to take place, which remains to the narrator a lifelong matter of regret. In "The Last of the Belles" the narrator has to give up not only on the girl but on the place that the South, which is the past itself, can retain in his memory. As noted, most of its traditions "are false." In certain other stories a marriage does take place but, as in "The Sensible Thing," unsolvable ambiguities remain. In the case of "The Third Casket," possibly to no one's surprise, the successful suitor is from the South. He has that largeness of character denied to his rivals, and he convinces both father and daughter that the Wall Street firm is better off when managed by someone who comes from outside "the most hard-boiled commercial age any country ever knew" (90). Just after Girard realizes how old he is, he gets renewed life—"twenty good years"—from his discovery of the virtues of the southern candidate. Both convince each other: the old man from the North admits that profit needs values, while his new partner and son-in-law admits that values need work. As a story, it is deeply unsatisfactory. The characters are there only in charcoal outline. But an idea that Fitzgerald took seriously is not obscured by trivialities of form.

In "Basil and Cleopatra" the Civil War is fought again, although when history repeats itself it takes the form of farce, with Littleboy Le Moyne disappearing under a pile of Yankee bodies at the battle of New Haven. When the South comes North in *The Great Gatsby*, we see a realistic permutation in the relationship of "innocent" Louisville and New York. In "The Third

Casket," in which North also marries South, a consummation occurs that in other stories may often be wished but never happens. This is a coda to all those other narratives in which the history of the republic is left as it actually was. The marriage of North and South is considerably more than a convenience of plot for Fitzgerald, and it speaks to more than his own marriage. It says a good deal about his view of American history, a history of alienation and disunion that mirrored and perhaps explained his sense of self. By far the majority of North–South marriages in Fitzgerald don't work or simply remain imperfect. This repeated story was useful in more than one way for Fitzgerald: as a revelation of his personal experience and also as an encoded representation of his sense of history. It is not a matter of correcting history through fiction. Freud's essay concludes—somewhat doctrinally—that art tries "to satisfy the wishes that reality does not satisfy."[36] That is usually the path not taken by Fitzgerald. From time to time he will think about themes of congruence and even of regeneration. But, in most cases, his map of the American scene is faithful to reality and not to wishes.

NOTES

1. See Scott Donaldson, "Scott Fitzgerald's Romance with the South," in *Southern Literary Journal* 5 (1973): 3–17; C. Hugh Holman, "Fitzgerald's Changes on the Southern Belle: The Tarleton Trilogy," in *The Short Stories of F. Scott Fitzgerald: New Approaches in Criticism*, ed. Jackson R. Buyer (Madison: University of Wisconsin Press, 1982), 53–64; Heidi Kunz Bullock, "The Southern and the Satirical in 'The Last of the Belles'" in *New Essays on F. Scott Fitzgerald's Neglected Stories*, ed. Jackson R. Buyer (Columbia: University of Missouri Press, 1996), 130–37.

2. For indispensable coverage of the North–South opposition in Fitzgerald see Frederick Wegener, "The 'Two Civil Wars' of F. Scott Fitzgerald," in *F. Scott Fitzgerald in the Twenty-First Century*, ed. Jackson R. Bryer, Ruth Prigozy, and Milton R. Stern (Tuscaloosa: University of Alabama Press, 2003), 238–66. This essay cites a large number of passages in Fitzgerald that would otherwise be difficult to find.

3. Robert Nisbet, "Progress," in *Prejudices: A Philosophical Dictionary* (Cambridge, Mass.: Harvard University Press, 1982), 241.

4. Charles A. and Mary R. Beard, *The Rise of American Civilization* (New York: Macmillan, 1927), 800.

5. Nisbet, "Progress," 241.

6. See Ronald Berman, "'The Diamond' and the Declining West," in *Fitzgerald, Hemingway, and the Twenties* (Tuscaloosa and London: University of Alabama Press, 2001), 40–51.

7. See Ronald Berman, *The Great Gatsby and Modern Times* (Urbana: University of Illinois Press, 1994), 59–81; *The Great Gatsby and Fitzgerald's World of Ideas* (Tuscaloosa and London: The University of Alabama Press, 1997), 44–67.

8. F. Scott Fitzgerald, *The Great Gatsby*, ed. Matthew J. Bruccoli (1925; repr., Cambridge: Cambridge University Press, 1991), 131. Future references in parentheses in my text.

9. In H. L. Mencken, *Prejudices, Fourth Series* (New York: Knopf, 1924). Mencken's essay "Totentanz" is listed under "Places to Live" in *A Second Mencken Chrestomathy*, ed. Terry Teachout (New York: Alfred A. Knopf, 1995), 179–86. Cited passages 181, 185.

10. H. L. Mencken, "Metropolis," in *A Second Mencken Chrestomathy*, 186–91. Cited passage 189. See also Mencken's column from the *Baltimore Evening Sun* of July 26, 1926, reprinted in *The Impossible H. L. Mencken: A Selection of His Best Newspaper Stories*, ed. Marion Elizabeth Rodgers (New York: Anchor Books, 1991), 110–11. The assumption of Metropolis, as seen in *Vanity Fair* and the *New Yorker*, is that it personifies style. But Mencken states that the charm of the city "chiefly issues out of money," which makes style possible.

11. Mencken, "Totentanz," 181.

12. Bruccoli, *The Short Stories of F. Scott Fitzgerald*, 97. Future references in parentheses in my text.

13. *A Preface to Morals* (New York: Macmillan, 1929), 232–39.

14. Lewis Mumford, "The City," in *Civilization in the United States*, ed. Harold E. Stearns (London: Jonathan Cape, 1922), 3–20. Cited passage 9.

15. See note 7.

16. It was an artifact on Fitzgerald's mind. He wrote of Sherwood Anderson that "what he takes to be only an empty tomato can" may be one of those "lesser things" that have been "endowed . . . with significance." "Sherwood Anderson on the Marriage Question," in *F. Scott Fitzgerald on Authorship*, ed. Matthew J. Bruccoli and Judith S. Baughman (Columbia: University of South Carolina Press, 1996), 83–85, especially 84.

17. Roland Marchand, *Advertising the American Dream* (Berkeley: University of California Press, 1986), 223. Images in the public realm rivaled categorical thought: "A well-placed radiant beam of light from a mysterious heavenly source might create a virtual halo around the advertised object without provoking the reader into outrage at the advertiser's presumption." These techniques of silence suggested patriotism, religion, and progress through a sequence of technological improvement (236–38).

18. Cited by Terry Teachout, *The Skeptic: A Life of H. L. Mencken* (New York: HarperCollins, 2002), 244. From "Little White Girl," *Scribner's*, April 1934, 78.

19. Alice Hall Petry, *Fitzgerald's Craft of Short Fiction* (Tuscaloosa and London: University of Alabama Press, 1989), 43.

20. See Fred Hobson, *Serpent in Eden: H. L. Mencken and the South* (Baton Rouge: Louisiana State University Press, 1978), 4: "It was in the field of *belles lettres* that Mencken's efforts were most noticeable. His notorious essay, the "Sahara," had been directed in particular at the literary poverty of the postbellum South." 21. Santayana, "Materialism and Idealism in American Life," in *Character and Opinion in the United States*, 109.

22. *Santayana on America*, ed. Richard Colton Lyon (New York: Harcourt, Brace & World, 1968), 207. From *The Idler and His Works* in 1957, but a continuation of Santayana's observations on national character since the 1900s. Emphasis added.

23. Stanley Brodwin, "F. Scott Fitzgerald and Willa Cather," in *F. Scott Fitzgerald in the Twenty-First Century*, 173–89. Cited passage 183.

24. C. Hugh Holman, "Fitzgerald's Changes on the Southern Belle," 55.

25. *The Golden Moment: The Novels of F. Scott Fitzgerald* (Urbana: University of Illinois Press, 1971), 253.

26. "Preface," *Civilization in the United States*, vii.

27. *William Faulkner: Toward Yoknapatawpha and Beyond* (New Haven: Yale University Press, 1979), 272. Frederick Wegener cites Fitzgerald on the personification of "the brilliant success of the North" and "the golden beauty of the South," *F. Scott Fitzgerald in the Twenty-First Century*, 252.

28. John O'Donnell, "Fitzgerald Condemns St. Paul Flappers: 'Unattractive, Selfish, Graceless,' Are Adjectives Applied to Middle West Girls," in *Conversations with F. Scott Fitzgerald*, 30–31. Cited passage 31. Originally published in the *St. Paul Daily News*, sec. 1, April 16, 1922.

29. F. Wilson, "F. Scott Fitzgerald Says: 'All Women Over Thirty-Five Should Be Murdered,'" in *Conversations with F. Scott Fitzgerald*, 55–59. Cited passage 57. Originally published in the *Metropolitan Magazine* 58 (November 1923): 34, 75–76.

30. *The Price Was High: The Last Uncollected Stories of F. Scott Fitzgerald*, ed. Matthew J. Bruccoli (New York: Harvest, 1979), 35. Future references in parentheses in my text.

31. *The Complete Works of Shakespeare*, ed. David Bevington (New York: HarperCollins, 1992), 185.

32. Sigmund Freud, *Writings on Art and Literature*, ed. Werner Hamacher and David E. Wellbury (Stanford: Stanford University Press, 1997), 109–21. The essay was translated into English in Freud's *Complete Psychological Works* of 1913.

33. Ibid., 120.

34. Ibid., 119.

35. Ibid., 120.

36. Ibid., 118.

SCOTT DONALDSON

Money and Marriage in Fitzgerald's Stories

I write about Love and Money; what else is there to write about?

—Jane Austen

I

Most authors constantly repeat themselves, Scott Fitzgerald observed in 1933. "We have two or three great and moving experiences in our lives," he continued, and on the basis of these experiences "we tell our two or three stories—each time in a new disguise—maybe ten times, maybe a hundred, as long as people will listen" (*My Lost City*, 86–87). One of the stories Fitzgerald told over and over again was about the struggle of the poor young man to win the hand of the rich girl. That had "always" been his situation, he remarked. He grew up "a poor boy in a rich town; a poor boy in a rich boy's school; a poor boy in a rich man's club at Princeton" (qtd. in Turnbull, *Fitzgerald*, 150).

He exaggerated his poverty. The Fitzgeralds were not badly off except in relation to the fabulously wealthy. But they did have less money than most families whose sons and daughters went to dancing school or college with Scott, and so he grew up thinking of himself as at a disadvantage in courting rich girls. Love and money became almost inextricably entangled in his mind and in his fiction. Almost everyone who has written about Fitzgerald has commented on his obsession with this topic, but usually they have

From *Fitzgerald & Hemingway: Works and Days*, pp. 107–18. Copyright © 2009 by Scott Donaldson.

concentrated on the novels, not the stories that reveal his changing attitudes toward money and marriage.

Rudolph Miller in "Absolution" (1924) suffers a "furious" attack of shame when he has no money for the church collection box, since Jeanne Brady, in the pew behind him, might notice (*Short Stories*, 268). In "Rags Martin-Jones and the Pr-nce of W-les" (1924), an imaginary merchant offers to sell the rich and beautiful Rags "some perfectly be-*oo*-tiful love," and he'll gladly send for a fresh supply since there's "so much money to spend" (*Short Stories*, 277). But if you don't have anything for the collection box, the girl will notice. And if you don't have enough to spend, the merchant will not bother. No money, no love. "If you haven't got money," Philip Dean instructs the hapless Gordon Sterrett in "May Day" (1920), "you've got to work and stay away from women" (*Short Stories*, 102).

Sterrett is a weakling who commits suicide when he wakes from a sodden drinking bout to find himself rejected by the society girl who used to love him and married to a "Jewel" of the lower classes. In this as in many other stories the poor young man engages in unequal combat with a wealthy competitor. "Remember," a precociously cynical Fitzgerald wrote at nineteen, "in all society nine girls out of ten marry for money and nine men out of ten are fools" (*Apprentice*, 126). He often felt discriminated against in such an environment. Occasionally he treated his predicament humorously:

> Those wealthy goats
> In raccoon coats
>   can wolf you away from me

he complained in "Oh, Sister, Can You Spare Your Heart," a jingle in his notebooks (*Notebooks*, 135). But such levity was rare, for he had been badly hurt.

Fitzgerald rang variations on the theme in his two best novels and in dozens of short stories. These were based—sometimes loosely, sometimes with almost photographic fidelity to the facts—on his love for two girls, Ginevra King and Zelda Sayre. Fitzgerald wooed Ginevra King of Chicago throughout 1915 and 1916, but she remained unwilling to commit herself to him. In August 1916, he went to visit her at her summer home in Lake Forest. "Once I thought that Lake Forest was the most glamorous place in the world," he wrote two decades later. "Maybe it was" (*Letters*, 84). As Ginevra's visiting beau, he escorted her to parties, dinners, and dances. But he also spent a "bad day at the McCormicks," endured a "Disappointment," and heard someone declare, "Poor boys shouldn't think of marrying rich girls" (*Ledger*, unpaginated). A few months later he and Ginevra broke up conclusively, but Fitzgerald did not soon stop caring about her.

Still, he fell in love with Zelda Sayre of Montgomery, Alabama, in September 1918, the month of Ginevra's wedding to William Mitchell ("beautiful Billy Mitchell," Fitzgerald had noted in his *Ledger* entry for August 1916). Zelda was widely known in Montgomery for her daring. Fitzgerald thought that "by temperament she was the most reckless" of all the women he ever knew. Nonetheless, Zelda "was cagey about throwing in her lot" with him before he had proved himself as a moneymaker. So at war's end Fitzgerald went off to New York, "the land of ambition and success," to make his fortune. When the fortune failed to develop, Zelda's devotion flagged; and after a desperate trip back to Montgomery, Fitzgerald boarded a Pullman car for her benefit and then sneaked back into the daycoach when the train got underway. In the summer of 1919 he gave up his job in New York, went west to St. Paul to rewrite *This Side of Paradise*, and in September learned that Scribner's would bring out his novel in the spring. In the meantime, he cranked out short stories and wired to the South such materialistic messages of love as "I HAVE SOLD THE MOVIE RIGHTS OF HEAD AND SHOULDERS TO THE METRO COMPANY FOR TWENTY-FIVE HUNDRED DOLLARS I LOVE YOU DEAREST GIRL" (Mizener, *The Far Side of Paradise*, 79–104).

"Essentially," Fitzgerald knew, "I got my public with stories of young love" (*Letters*, 128). And in the stories he began selling to the *Saturday Evening Post* in 1919 and 1920 it was almost always young love in high society. As early as New Year's Eve of 1920, he was complaining to Maxwell Perkins that he'd "go mad if I have to do another debutante, which is what they want" (*Letters*, 145). Readers started a Fitzgerald story not always sure of a happy ending, but with confidence that he would provide a glimpse of a glamorous social world few of them had ever inhabited. So stereotyped was this social setting that his illustrators usually presented the characters as handsome creatures in full evening dress. The men wore tuxedos or tails, the women gowns, though there might be no reason whatever on the basis of the story for them to be so attired. In "The Bowl" (1928), for example, the male protagonist is described as customarily wearing tan or soft gray suits with black ties. Yet in the illustrations he appears in formal evening clothes.

Fitzgerald's novels of love and money usually attack the rich. The Buchanans treat Jay Gatsby brutally, then escape while his dream and life blood ebb away. The Warrens retain Doctor Diver until they've used up his vitality, then dismiss him. The stories are less consistent in their attitude toward the wealthy, yet most of them can be classified as falling within one of two strains. One group of stories depicts the success, or seeming success, of the poor young man in wooing the rich girl. In the other, more effective group, the young man is rejected in his quest or if successful is subsequently disappointed.

The usual trouble with stories of the first kind is that they are not persuasive. At least subconsciously, Fitzgerald must have realized this, for he often tricked out such tales with fantasy or with outrageous challenges to reader disbelief. "The Offshore Pirate" (1920) provides a case in point. As the first sentence declares, it tells the "unlikely story" of the winning of Ardita Farnam, a yellow-haired embodiment of the golden girl. Ardita is bored by the predictable round of her social life, and eager, so she says, to cast her lot with anyone who will show some imagination. That someone turns out to be Toby Moreland, a rich boy playing at poverty. He attracts her interest by pretending to be a musician who has risen to wealth first by way of his talent, then by stealing the jewels of society matrons. He commandeers Ardita's yacht but though fascinated, she withholds her hand:

> "We can get married in Callao."
> "What sort of life can you offer me? I don't mean that unkindly, but seriously, what would become of me if the people who want that twenty-thousand-dollar reward ever catch up with you?" (*SHORT STORIES*, 90)

It would be different if she were "a little, poor girl dreaming over a fence in a warm cow country" and he, newly rich with ill-gotten gains, had come along to astonish her with his munificence. Then she'd stare into the windows of the jewelry store and want the "big oblong watch that's platinum and has diamonds all round the edge" but would decide "it was too expensive and choose one of white gold for a hundred dollars." And he'd say, "Expensive? I should say not!" and "pretty soon the platinum one would be gleaming" on her wrist (*Short Stories*, 90). She wishes it were that way, but it isn't, so Ardita turns her suitor down until, at the end, she finds to her relief that he is both imaginative *and* extremely wealthy. A rich boy may charm his girl by pretending to have been poor, like Toby Moreland and like George Van Tyne in "The Unspeakable Egg" (1924), who wins his Fifi by playing the role of a bearded, disheveled roustabout (*The Price Was High*, 126–42). But of course it does not work the other way around.

A good many Fitzgerald stories hinge upon an actual rather than imaginary reversal of fortune. In these tales, he posits an America where the ambitious, hard-working lad rises to receive the romantic reward due him. Generally, stories that conform to this "boy makes money, gets girl" pattern are among the worst Fitzgerald ever wrote. They tend to be overplotted to the point where manipulation of character and circumstance becomes obvious. They lack verisimilitude and conviction. Commenting on two such stories—"Presumption" and "The Adolescent Marriage"—written in the fall and winter of 1925 and 1926, Robert Sklar observes that the author of *The Great Gatsby* had "put his matured art and intellectual perception into the requirements of slick magazine stories . . . as if he were an adolescent boy forced to wear short pants" (Sklar, *Fitzgerald*, 215–16).

In "Presumption," the more interesting of the two, Juan Chandler pursues a rich debutante, Noel Garneau. Juan comes from middle-class circumstances in Akron and swims beyond his depth in the social waters of Culpepper Bay. "You're not in any position to think anything serious about Noel Garneau" (*The Price Was High*, 187), his cousin Cora reminds him, and Noel does in fact reject him at first, though only partly because of his relative poverty. Juan really loses his chance when he foolishly tries to make her jealous. He can contemplate only one way to remedy the situation: by making a proper fortune. "I haven't any money and I'm in love with a girl who has," he confesses to a golfing partner who turns out, by the sort of coincidence that makes these stories embarrassing, to be Noel's father. Mr. Garneau advises Juan to stick it out.

> "Does the girl care about you?" he inquired.
> "Yes."
> "Well, go after her, young man. All the money in the world hasn't been made by a long shot." (*THE PRICE WAS HIGH*, 189)

Driven by these words of encouragement, Juan drops out of college to get wealthy, and eighteen months later he presents himself to Noel as a rich young man. Though she is now engaged, he follows her from Boston to New York, where he presents his case to her aunt, the soignée Mrs. Poindexter:

> "I've been called presumptuous in this matter, and perhaps to some extent I am. Perhaps all poor boys who are in love with wealthy girls are presumptuous. But it happens that I am no longer a poor boy, and I have good reason to believe that Noel cares for me." (*THE PRICE WAS HIGH*, 200)

Here, as Sklar points out, Fitzgerald reworks the *Gatsby* plot, and when Juan reads the note Noel has left directing her aunt to dismiss the "intolerable bore" who is pursuing her with his "presumptuous whining," he assumes all is lost. Juan then realized, Fitzgerald writes, "that fundamentally they were all akin—Cousin Cora, Noel, her father, this cold, lovely woman here [her mother]—affirming the prerogative of the rich to marry always within their caste, to erect artificial barriers and standards against those who could presume upon a summer's philandering" (*The Price Was High*, 201). The words could hardly ring truer. But wait! It's a case of mistaken identity, and the bore Noel speaks of is Mr. *Templeton*, the man she'd been engaged to, and she'll be delighted to see and fall in love with and marry the newly rich Mr. *Chandler*.

"Presumption" ran as the lead story in the January 9, 1926, *Saturday Evening Post*. Like all of Fitzgerald's work, it has its moments. But along with "The Adolescent Marriage" (1926) and such later *Post* publications as "The Rubber Check" (1932), "More Than Just a House" (1933), and "The Family Bus" (1933), it fails for lack of emotional conviction. John O'Hara wrote Fitzgerald admiring his portrait of Lew Lowrie, the "climber" in "More Than Just a House." He always did the "climber" well, O'Hara told him, and rightly so, for Fitzgerald the author felt a natural sympathy for the poor young man on the make. But as he grew older, he could no longer care passionately whether his young man won the golden girl. Although the magazines wanted him to continue turning out commercial love stories, by the early 1930s he was losing interest in such "inessential and specious matters" and could no longer write them convincingly (Turnbull, *Fitzgerald*, 300).

Occasionally Fitzgerald shifted the sexes as a variation on his basic theme. Thus in such early stories as "Myra Meets His Family" (1920) and "The Popular Girl" (1922), a poor girl sets her cap for a rich boy. The author's sympathy switches to the woman in this situation; Fitzgerald will not or cannot identify with the rich young man. At twenty-one, Myra Harper "can still get any man she wants," and she wants Knowleton Whitney: "You know what a wiz he is on looks, and his father's worth a fortune, they say. . . . He's smart as a whip, and shy—rather sweetly shy—and they say his family has the best-looking place in Westchester County" (*The Price Was High*, 13–14). Warned about Myra's reputation as a gold digger, Whitney invites her to the mansion where he tests her devotion by introducing her to awful people (actors hired for the occasion) masquerading as his parents. He soon confesses his plot, but Myra still exacts her revenge by staging a phony wedding and leaving him cold immediately afterward. The rich boy is bested, albeit rather cruelly. In "The Popular Girl," Fitzgerald settles for a more conventional happy ending. Yanci Bowman pretends to a wealth and social position that will, she thinks, impress her rich beau. But he loves her, not her background, and once she has spent her last dime they blissfully ride into Manhattan—and the future—together.

II

Fitzgerald's tales of rejection and disappointment are far more effective than those where true love unpersuasively conquers all. They are more deeply felt, more true to the life. The stories of rejection also serve to demonstrate the author's growing maturity of outlook, his disturbing sense that pursuit and capture of the golden girl was not really worth all the trouble and heartache. He felt anything but philosophical about the matter when he wrote *This Side of Paradise*, however. The section of that novel called "The Debutante"—really a short story in the form of a playlet, with dialogue and stage directions—painfully relives Fitzgerald's rejection by Ginevra King.

Initially Rosalind Connage, the debutante, agrees to marry Amory Blaine when he's "ready" for her, despite the fact that he's making a paltry thirty-five dollars a week. But soon she changes her mind, choosing a rich suitor instead. "I don't want to think about pots and kitchens and brooms. I want to worry whether my legs will get slick and brown in the summer" (183), she explains. Her selfishness is appalling, but Fitzgerald will not condemn her. In a concluding stage direction, he assigns Rosalind a capacity for feeling like his own: "(*And deep under the aching sadness that will pass in time, Rosalind feels that she has lost something, she knows not what, she knows not why*)" (184).

A decade later Fitzgerald reworked the same material in "A Snobbish Story" (1930), showing much less sympathy for the rich girl involved. In this story as in four others of 1930 and 1931, she is Josephine Perry, Lake Forest debutante. Josephine becomes attracted to John Bailey, a *Chicago Tribune* reporter and aspiring playwright, but Bailey comes from Bohemia, not the upper-class suburbs, and has a wife who lives apart from him. He casts Josephine as the lead in his play, called *Race Riot*, and comes to the Perrys' home to interest her father in backing the production. While he's there, a policeman appears with the disturbing news that Bailey's wife has tried to take her life. Bailey thereupon disappears, while Mr. and Mrs. Perry chastise their daughter about consorting with "people like that" who had no business upsetting the decorum of Lake Forest.

Josephine accepts their criticism and determines that she will no longer involve herself with potential trouble. She decides that "any value she might have was in the immediate, shimmering present—and thus thinking, she threw in her lot with the rich and powerful of the world forever" (Basil 269). Thereafter she falls victim to what Fitzgerald, in the title of another of his stories about her, calls "Emotional Bankruptcy." While Rosalind Connage had supposedly been tenderhearted, though hardheaded on the question of marriage, Josephine Perry becomes equally tough of heart and head. The difference lies not in the girl who sat for both portraits but in Fitzgerald's perception of that girl and the nature of the struggle to win her hand. In his better stories of the 1920s, he gradually deromanticized the girl and deemphasized the glory of the quest.

The rich girl is still vibrant as Judy Jones in the great "Winter Dreams" (1922). Dexter Green, the poor young man in the story, commits himself to pursuing her with an abundant supply of ambition and energy. He feels driven to possess not only Judy but everything she represents: "He wanted not association with glittering things and glittering people—he wanted the glittering things themselves. Often he reached out for the best without knowing why he wanted it—and sometimes he ran up against the mysterious denials and prohibitions in which life indulges" (*Short Stories*, 220–21). To get Judy's attention, he manages to make a success of himself, and, as he had hoped, his ability to earn money dramatically transforms their relationship. On their first dinner date, she confesses that she's had "a terrible afternoon. There was a man I cared about, and this afternoon he told me out of a clear sky that he was poor as a church-mouse." Her interest in him, she confesses, had not been strong enough to stand the shock. Then this dialogue ensues:

> "Let's start right," she interrupted herself suddenly. "Who are you, anyhow?"
> For a moment Dexter hesitated. Then:
> "I'm nobody," he announced. "My career is largely a matter of futures."
> "Are you poor?"
> "No," he said frankly. "I'm probably making more money than any man my age in the Northwest. I know that's an obnoxious remark, but you advised me to start right."
> There was a pause. Then she smiled and the corners of her mouth drooped and an almost imperceptible sway brought her closer to him, looking up into his eyes.

And then they kiss, her kisses "like charity, creating want by holding back nothing at all" (*Short Stories*, 226). But Dexter does not win the girl after all, and at the end of the story he is shocked and disillusioned to hear Judy spoken of as "faded" and "a little too old" for her husband in Detroit (234).

The loss of romantic illusions forms a central motif in stories of this type. Jonquil Cary in "'The Sensible Thing'" (1924) fends off the proposal of George O'Kelly until he is "ready" for her. This code word, also used by Rosalind to Amory and by Zelda to Scott, meant that the suitor must first establish himself financially. Until he did so, she would remain "nervous" (another code word used by both the fictional Jonquil and the real Zelda) about the prospect of marriage. Heeding the message, the ambitious O'Kelly strikes out for South America, makes his pile, and returns to claim his girl. But some of the magic has gone: "as he kissed her he knew that though he search through eternity he could never recapture those lost April hours. . . . There are all kinds of love in the world, but never the same love twice" (*Short Stories*, 301).

A still bitterer disillusionment awaited some of those who—like George O'Kelly—eventually win the girl. Then they are liable to find, as in "Gretchen's Forty Winks" (1924) and "The Adjuster" (1925), that they have married creatures of exquisite irresponsibility and selfishness. What's more, Fitzgerald implies that the possession of money and the idle hours that come with it encourage adultery. Luella Hemper in "The Adjuster" is bored. She "honestly wanted something to do. If she had a little more money and a little less love, she could have gone in for horses or for vagarious amour. Or if they had a little less money, her surplus energy would have been absorbed by hope and even by effort" (*Six Tales*, 142). But she falls in between and concentrates instead on making her husband's life miserable.

Money also confers a license for misbehavior on Anson Hunter in Fitzgerald's brilliant "The Rich Boy" (1926). Anson feels no more compunction about breaking hearts than about getting drunk. When caught in a compromising situation he simply refuses to apologize. But Anson pays deeply for his privileges, since he is unable to commit himself to any one woman, even to the one he thought he loved. His financial capacity is balanced by an emotional incapacity. The rich boy cannot give, only receive. Fitzgerald bids him adieu with this reflection:

> I don't think he was ever happy unless some one was in love with him, responding to him like filings to a magnet, helping him to explain himself, promising him something. What it was I do not know. Perhaps they promised that there would always be women who would spend their brightest, freshest, rarest hours to nurse and protect that superiority he cherished in his heart. (SHORT STORIES, 349)

Fitzgerald's mature view of the relationship between love and money is that too much money militates against true love. Such wealth is destructive because "those who have it lose the capacity to feel for others" (Kennedy, "Are Our Novelists Hostile," 33). This is true of the Buchanans and the Warrens of his novels, the Anson Hunters and Josephine Perrys of his stories. In this respect, the young man on the rise holds an emotional advantage over both his rich competitors and the golden girl he is pursuing.

The story that best illustrates Fitzgerald's altered perception of this relationship is "The Bridal Party," published in the *Saturday Evening Post* on August 9, 1930. On the surface this appears to be yet another tale about the poor boy losing the girl to another, much better-off young man. Michael Curly comes to Paris where he runs across Caroline Dandy and her fiancé, Hamilton Rutherford. As Michael remembers,

> He had met Caroline Dandy when she was seventeen, possessed her young heart all through her first season in New York, and then lost her, slowly, tragically, uselessly, because he had no money and could make no money; because, with all the energy and good will in the world, he could not find himself; because, loving him still, Caroline had lost faith and begun to see him as something pathetic, futile and shabby, outside the great, shining stream of life toward which she was inevitably drawn. (*SHORT STORIES*, 561–62)

Her "entire clan," Michael believes, had aligned themselves against him: "What a little counter he was in this game of families and money!" (563).

In Paris, though, Michael unexpectedly comes into an inheritance and resolves to take up his courtship once again. And again he fails, though not for lack of resources. Caroline prefers Rutherford for his solidity and decisiveness, she tells Michael. "It was that more than the question of . . . money" (566). She proves the point by sticking with Rutherford when he discovers, on the night of his stag party, that he has lost every cent he's made and must start over.

Michael goes to their wedding expecting to feel sorrow. But his own financial windfall combines with champagne and the "ceremonial function" to obliterate the pain. "All the bitterness melted out of him suddenly and the world reconstituted itself out of the youth and happiness that was all around him, profligate as the spring sunshine." Yet though "cured" of his sorrow, Michael may also be "cured," the last sentence suggests, of ever feeling so deeply again. "He was trying to remember which one of the bridesmaids he had made a date to dine with tonight as he walked forward to bid Hamilton and Caroline Rutherford good-by" (576).

Through its ironic view of the narrator-protagonist, "The Bridal Party" repudiates the belief, often implied and sometimes articulated in Fitzgerald's early fiction, that money could purchase almost anything or anybody one wanted to buy. To young Dalyrimple, returning from World War I, it seemed that "happiness was what he wanted—a slowly rising scale of gratifications of the normal appetites—and he had a strong conviction that the materials, if not the inspiration of happiness, could be bought with money" (*Flappers*, 166). Fitzgerald wrote "Dalyrimple Goes Wrong" in 1920. A decade later, in such stories as "The Bridal Party," "The Swimmers" (1929), and "Babylon Revisited" (1931), he demonstrated the relative impotence of money.

Henry Marston of "The Swimmers" is deceived by his French wife, Choupette, and seeks to keep custody of their children while divorcing her. His wife's lover, an aggressive American businessman named Wiese, tells

Marston that he has no chance, that Wiese's money will insure that the children remain with Choupette. "Money is power," Wiese insists. "Money made this country, built its great and glorious cities, created its industries, covered it with an iron network of railroads. It's money that harnesses the forces of Nature, creates the machine and makes it go when money says go, and stop when money says stop" (*Short Stories*, 508). As if to illustrate how wrong he is, the motorboat in which Wiese delivers this speech sputters to a halt, and they are drifting out to sea, apparently at the mercy of the Atlantic, when Marston, the only swimmer of the three, agrees to swim for help in return for custody of the children. Skill and knowledge carry the day. For Marston as for Fitzgerald, it was not money but "a willingness of the heart" (512) that defined America.

"Babylon Revisited," one of Fitzgerald's best stories, also focuses on the issue of child custody. During the boom of the 1920s, Charlie Wales got rich and then wasted his time in drinking and lost his wife to illness. Charlie was so badly off when his wife died that her sister and brother-in-law assumed care of Honoria, the Waleses' daughter. When the boom turned to bust, a reformed Charlie comes to Paris to try to get Honoria back. At the end he finds he cannot yet gain custody of her and reflects with bitter irony on the days and nights when it seemed that one could purchase forgetfulness, when a man could lock his wife out in the snow (as he had done) "because the snow of twenty-nine wasn't real snow. If you didn't want it to be snow, you just paid some money" (*Short Stories*, 633). Charlie's money seems to him to have been as much a handicap as a blessing, however. His wife's sister still resents the profligate way Charlie threw his money around after making a killing in the stock market of the 1920s. Now that he has lost that fortune and started to build another anew, he alienates her again by announcing how well he's doing. Nor can he, yet, entirely shake free of the drunken companions his money had enabled him to dissipate away his life with a few years before. So he must wait still longer for Honoria, the only girl left for him. In the meantime he can only "send her a lot of things," though, he thinks in anger, that "was just money—he had given so many people money" (633).

In the mid-1920s, Jacob Booth, the hero of "Jacob's Ladder" (1927), made $800,000 in real estate. Then "he had tried—tried hard—for a year and a half to marry one of the richest women in America" (*Short Stories*, 353). If he had loved her, he could have had her. But Jacob did not love her; he pursued her because of the glitter of wealth that surrounded her. A similar halo hovered in the vicinity of many of the rich girls Fitzgerald's young men were forever pursuing in his stories of the 1920s. But during his last years as a writer, he rarely sent his male characters out in quest of the golden girl. He had learned by then that the halo was slightly tarnished and the glitter not always gold. He had also discovered that there were other things as powerful as money and that having excessive wealth rarely worked to the benefit of those who possessed it. Besides, by then he had told his recurring story of money and marriage—sometimes in pedestrian fashion, sometimes superlatively well—often enough.

Chronology

1896	Born Francis Scott Key Fitzgerald on September 24 in St. Paul, Minnesota, to Edward Fitzgerald and Mary McQuillan Fitzgerald.
1911	Attends the Newman School, a Catholic boarding school in Hackensack, New Jersey.
1913	Matriculates at Princeton. Works on productions for the university's amateur theatrical company, the Triangle Club.
1917	Leaves Princeton without receiving a degree. Joins the U.S. Army as a second lieutenant and goes for training at Fort Leavenworth, Kansas.
1918	Completes his first novel, *The Romantic Egotist*. Meets Zelda Sayre when transferred to Camp Sheridan, Montgomery, Alabama. In October *The Romantic Egotist* is rejected by Scribner's.
1919	After being discharged from the Army, moves to New York, works as a copywriter for an advertising agency. In July returns to the familial home in St. Paul. Begins revising *The Romantic Egotist*. Under its new title, *This Side of Paradise*, the book is accepted by Scribner's in September.
1920	*This Side of Paradise* published in March. Marries Zelda Sayre on April 3. In September Scribner's publishes *Flappers and Philosophers*, a collection of stories.
1921	Daughter Frances Scott Fitzgerald born on October 26.

1922	*The Beautiful and Damned* published by Scribner's in March. The short story "The Diamond as Big as the Ritz" appears in the *Smart Set* in June. *Tales of the Jazz Age*, a second story collection, published by Scribner's in September.
1925	*The Great Gatsby* published by Scribner's.
1926	A third collection of stories, *All the Sad Young Men*, published by Scribner's.
1927	Spends two months in Hollywood writing scripts for United Artists.
1930	Zelda has nervous breakdown while traveling in Europe.
1931	"Babylon Revisited" published in *The Saturday Evening Post*.
1932	Zelda suffers from a second breakdown, after which she is committed to a psychiatric clinic in Baltimore. She is discharged in June and her novel, *Save Me the Waltz*, is published the same year.
1934	Writes short stories in a desperate attempt to repay his debts after *Tender Is the Night* appears to disappointing sales. Suffers nervous breakdown in June.
1935	Declining physical health attributed to heavy drinking. Recuperates in Asheville, North Carolina.
1936	"The Crack-Up" essays appear in *Esquire* magazine. Zelda sent to a sanitarium in Asheville, where she remains until her death.
1937	Moves to Hollywood to work as a scriptwriter for MGM. Begins a relationship with Sheilah Graham.
1940	"Pat Hobby" stories published in *Esquire*. Dies from a heart attack on December 21.
1941	*The Last Tycoon*, an unfinished novel, published by Scribner's.
1945	*The Crack-Up*, edited by Edmund Wilson, published by New Directions.
1948	Zelda dies in a fire at the sanitarium in Asheville.

Contributors

HAROLD BLOOM is Sterling Professor of the Humanities at Yale University. Educated at Cornell and Yale universities, he is the author of more than 30 books, including *Shelley's Mythmaking* (1959), *Blake's Apocalypse* (1963), *Yeats* (1970), *The Anxiety of Influence* (1973), *A Map of Misreading* (1975), *Kabbalah and Criticism* (1975), *Agon: Toward a Theory of Revisionism* (1982), *The American Religion* (1992), *The Western Canon* (1994), *Omens of Millennium: The Gnosis of Angels, Dreams, and Resurrection* (1996), *Shakespeare: The Invention of the Human* (1998), *How to Read and Why* (2000), *Genius: A Mosaic of One Hundred Exemplary Creative Minds* (2002), *Hamlet: Poem Unlimited* (2003), *Where Shall Wisdom Be Found?* (2004), *Jesus and Yahweh: The Names Divine* (2005), and *Till I End My Song: A Gathering of Last Poems* (2010). In addition, he is the author of hundreds of articles, reviews, and editorial introductions. In 1999, Professor Bloom received the American Academy of Arts and Letters' Gold Medal for Criticism. He has also received the International Prize of Catalonia, the Alfonso Reyes Prize of Mexico, and the Hans Christian Andersen Bicentennial Prize of Denmark.

KENNETH G. JOHNSTON is the author of *The Tip of the Iceberg: Hemingway and the Short Story*.

WILLIAM J. BRONDELL is an associate professor emeritus of Kansas State University. He taught courses in old English, the short story, and fiction and film.

LEONARD PODIS is a professor at Oberlin College. He coauthored *Rethinking Writing* and *Writing: Invention, Form, and Style*, as well as other titles.

ROBERT ROULSTON taught at Murray State University. He coauthored *The Winding Road to West Egg: The Artistic Development of F. Scott Fitzgerald.*

BRUCE L. GRENBERG is retired as an associate professor at the University of British Columbia. He is the author of *Some Other World to Find: Quest and Negation in the Works of Herman Melville* and has written for the *Fitzgerald/Hemingway Annual* and other publications.

J. GERALD KENNEDY is a professor at Louisiana State University. He is the coeditor of *French Connections: Hemingway and Fitzgerald Abroad* and directed the Hemingway/Fitzgerald International Conference in Paris. He is the author of *Imagining Paris: Exile, Writing, and American Identity.*

RICHARD ALLAN DAVISON is a retired professor of the University of Delaware. He has published books on Charles and Kathleen Norris and more than 60 articles in numerous journals.

VERONICA MAKOWSKY is a professor and director of graduate studies, Storrs campus, at the University of Connecticut. She has contributed to *Approaches to Teaching F. Scott Fitzgerald's* The Great Gatsby; she edited Blackmur's *Studies in Henry James* and has published other titles and articles as well. She has been the editor of *MELUS.*

RONALD BERMAN is an emeritus professor at the University of California, San Diego. His publications include *Fitzgerald, Hemingway, and the Twenties*, and *Fitzgerald-Wilson-Hemingway.*

SCOTT DONALDSON is an emeritus professor of the College of William and Mary. His work includes *Fool for Love, F. Scott Fitzgerald* and *Hemingway vs. Fitzgerald: The Rise and Fall of a Literary Friendship.* He is the editor of *Critical Essays on F. Scott Fitzgerald's "The Great Gatsby"* and other titles.

Bibliography

Abramson, Edward A. "Aliens, Stereotypes, and Social Change: The Jews and Hollywood in F. Scott Fitzgerald's Fiction." *Studies in American Jewish Literature* 24 (2005): 116–36.

Assadi, Jamal, and William Freedman, ed. *A Distant Drummer: Foreign Perspectives on F. Scott Fitzgerald.* New York: Peter Lang, 2007.

Berman, Ronald. *Fitzgerald, Hemingway, and the Twenties.* Tuscaloosa: University of Alabama Press, 2001.

———. *Translating Modernism: Fitzgerald and Hemingway.* Tuscaloosa: University of Alabama Press, 2009.

Bloom, Harold, ed. *F. Scott Fitzgerald.* New York: Chelsea House Publishers, 2006.

Bouzonviller, Elizabeth. "A Decisive Stopover in 'an Antiseptic Smelling Land': Switzerland as a Place of Decision and Recovery in F. Scott Fitzgerald's Fiction." *F. Scott Fitzgerald Review* 3 (2004): 27–42.

Brown, Judith. *Glamour in Six Dimensions: Modernism and the Radiance of Form.* Ithaca, N.Y.: Cornell University Press, 2009.

Bruccoli, Matthew J. *F. Scott Fitzgerald: A Descriptive Bibliography.* Revised edition. Pittsburgh: Pittsburgh University Press, 1988.

Claridge, Henry, ed. *F. Scott Fitzgerald: Critical Assessments.* 4 vols. Near Robertsbridge, UK: Helm Information, 1991.

Cole, A. Fletcher. "'Fairways of His Imagination': Golf and Social Status in F. Scott Fitzgerald's Fiction." In *Upon Further Review: Sports in American Literature,* edited by Michael Cocchiarale and Scott D. Emmert, pp. 75–85. Westport, Conn.: Praeger, 2004.

Cowart, David. "'Babylon Revisited': The Tragedy of Charlie Wales." *Journal of the Short Story in English* 3 (Autumn 1984): 21–28.

Cowley, Malcolm. "The Scott Fitzgerald Story." *New Republic* 124 (February 12, 1951): 17–20.

Curnutt, Kirk. *The Cambridge Introduction to F. Scott Fitzgerald*. Cambridge, UK; New York: Cambridge University Press, 2007.

Curnutt, Kirk, ed. *A Historical Guide to F. Scott Fitzgerald*. Oxford; New York: Oxford University Press, 2004.

Daniels, Thomas E. "Toward a Definitive Edition of F. Scott Fitzgerald's Short Stories." *Papers of the Bibliographical Society of America* 71 (1977): 295–310.

de Koster, Katie, ed. *Readings on F. Scott Fitzgerald*. San Diego: Greenhaven Press, 1998.

Forter, Greg. "F. Scott Fitzgerald, Psychobiography, and the Fin-de-Siècle Crisis in Masculinity." In *Desire of the Analysts: Psychoanalysis and Cultural Criticism*, edited by Greg Forter and Paul Allen Miller, pp. 147–175. Albany: State University of New York Press, 2008.

Gallo, Rose Adrienne. *F. Scott Fitzgerald*. New York: F. Ungar, 1978.

Gross, Seymour L. "Fitzgerald's 'Babylon Revisited.'" *College English* 25, no. 2 (November 1963): 128–35.

Gruber, Michael P. "Fitzgerald's 'May Day': A Prelude to Triumph." *Essays in Literature* 2, no. 1 (1973): 20–35.

Higgins, John A. *F. Scott Fitzgerald: A Study of the Stories*. Jamaica, N.Y.: St. John's University Press, 1971.

Hunt, Jan. "The Evasion of Adult Love in Fitzgerald's Fiction." *Centennial Review* 17 (1973): 152–69.

Jett, Kevin. "Overturning the Verdict: Revisiting Fitzgerald's Charlie Wales." *Lamar Journal of the Humanities* 23, no. 2 (Fall 1997): 5–19.

Kennedy, J. Gerald. "Poe, Fitzgerald, and the American Nightmare." *Edgar Allan Poe Review* 5, no. 2 (Fall 2004): 4–14.

Kumar, Sukrita Paul. *Man, Woman, and Androgyny: A Study of the Novels of Theodore Dreiser, Scott Fitzgerald, and Ernest Hemingway*. New Delhi: Indus, 1989.

Lee, Robert A., ed. *Scott Fitzgerald: The Promises of Life*. London: Vision; New York: St. Martin's Press, 1989.

LeGates, Charlotte. "Dual-Perspective Irony and the Fitzgerald Short Story." *Iowa English Bulletin: Yearbook* 26, no. 7 (1977): 18–20.

Lehan, Richard. *F. Scott Fitzgerald and the Craft of Fiction*. Carbondale; Southern Illinois University Press, 1966.

Lowe-Evans, Mary. *Catholic Nostalgia in Joyce and Company*. Gainesville: University Press of Florida, 2008.

Mangum, Bryant. *A Fortune Yet: Money in the Art of F. Scott Fitzgerald's Short Stories*. New York: Garland; 1991.

Mazzella, Anthony J. "The Tension of Opposites in Fitzgerald's 'May Day.'" *Studies in Short Fiction* 14 (1977): 379–85.

McDonald, Jarom Lyle. *Sports, Narrative, and Nation in the Fiction of F. Scott Fitzgerald*. New York: Routledge, 2007.

———. "What a Play: The Rhetoric of Football in Fitzgerald's Short Fiction." *F. Scott Fitzgerald Review* 2 (2003): 134–55.

Miller, James E. Jr. *F. Scott Fitzgerald, His Art and His Technique*. New York: New York University Press, 1964.

Mizener, Arthur, ed. *F. Scott Fitzgerald, a Collection of Critical Essays*. Englewood Cliffs, N.J.: Prentice-Hall, 1963.

Morioka, Sakae. "Scott Fitzgerald's Short Stories." *Kyushu University Studies in English Language and Literature* 11 (1961): 1–18.

Nowlin, Michael. *F. Scott Fitzgerald's Racial Angles and the Business of Literary Greatness*. New York: Palgrave Macmillan, 2007.

Pelzer, Linda C. *Student Companion to F. Scott Fitzgerald*. Westport, Conn.: Greenwood Press, 2000.

Perlis, Alan. "The Narrative Is All: A Study of F. Scott Fitzgerald's 'May Day.'" *Western Humanities Review* 33 (1979): 65–72.

Perosa, Sergio. *The Art of F. Scott Fitzgerald*, trans. Charles Metz and Sergio Perosa. Ann Arbor: University of Michigan Press, 1965.

Petry, Alice Hall. *Fitzgerald's Craft of Short Fiction: The Collected Stories, 1920–1935*. Ann Arbor: UMI Research Press, 1989.

Piper, Henry Dan. *F. Scott Fitzgerald, a Critical Portrait*. New York: Holt, Rinehart and Winston, 1965.

Prigozy, Ruth, ed. *The Cambridge Companion to F. Scott Fitzgerald*. Cambridge, England: Cambridge University Press, 2002.

Rand, William E. "The Structure of the Outsider in the Short Fiction of Richard Wright and F. Scott Fitzgerald." *College Language Association Journal* 40, no. 2 (December 1996): 230–45.

Raubicheck, Walter. "Hollywood Nights: The Filmmaker as Artist in 'Crazy Sunday.'" *F. Scott Fitzgerald Review* 7 (2009): 53–64.

Roulston, Robert, and Helen H. Roulston. *The Winding Road to West Egg: The Artistic Development of F. Scott Fitzgerald*. Lewisburg, Pa.: Bucknell University Press; London: Associated University Presses, 1995.

Schlacks, Deborah Davis. *American Dream Visions: Chaucer's Surprising Influence on F. Scott Fitzgerald*. New York: Peter Lang, 1994.

Selley, April. "Lacking the Pap of Wonder: The Search for Mothers in *The Great Gatsby* and Fitzgerald's Short Stories." *Revista Portuguesa de Estudos Anglo-Americanos* 2 (1992): 47–59.

Way, Brian. *F. Scott Fitzgerald and the Art of Social Fiction*. New York: St. Martin's Press, 1980.

Weston, Elizabeth A. *The International Theme in F. Scott Fitzgerald's Literature*. New York: P. Lang, 1995.

Acknowledgments

Kenneth G. Johnston, "Fitzgerald's 'Crazy Sunday': Cinderella in Hollywood." From *Literature/Film Quarterly* 6 (1978): 214–21. Copyright © 1978 by Salisbury University.

William J. Brondell, "Structural Metaphors in Fitzgerald's Short Fiction." From *Kansas Quarterly* 14, no. 2 (Spring 1982): 95–114. Copyright © 1982 by *Kansas Quarterly*.

Leonard A. Podis, "Fitzgerald's 'The Diamond as Big as the Ritz' and Hawthorne's 'Rappaccini's Daughter.'" From *Studies of Short Fiction* 21, no. 3 (Summer 1984): 243–50. Copyright © Newberry College.

Robert Roulston, "Fitzgerald's 'May Day': The Uses of Irresponsibility." From *Modern Fiction Studies* 34, no. 2 (Summer 1988): 207–15. Copyright © 1988 by the Johns Hopkins University Press.

Bruce L. Grenberg, "'Outside the Cabinet-Maker's': Fitzgerald's 'Ode to a Nightingale.'" From *New Essays on F. Scott Fitzgerald's Forgotten Stories,* edited and with an introduction by Jackson R. Bryer. Copyright © 1996 by the Curators of the University of Missouri.

J. Gerald Kennedy, "Figuring the Damage: Fitzgerald's 'Babylon Revisited' and Hemingway's 'The Snows of Kilimanjaro.'" From *French Connections: Hemingway and Fitzgerald Abroad,* edited by J. Gerald Kennedy and Jackson R. Bryer.

143

Index

Characters in literary works are indexed by first name (if any), followed by the name of the work in parentheses